MODERNIZATION IN CHINA: THE EFFECTS ON ITS PEOPLE AND ECONOMIC DEVELOPMENT

Beijing Youth Daily & Youth Humanities and Social Science Research Center of the Chinese Academy of Social Sciences

Foreign Languages Press

First Edition 2004

Translated by: Liang Faming   Hao Guangfeng
            Kong Wei   Cong Guoling   Lu Jiang
English text edited by: Foster Stockwell   Huang Youyi

Home Page:
http://www.flp.com.cn
E-mail Addresses:
info@flp.com.cn
sales@flp.com.cn

ISBN 7-119-03297-6
© Foreign Languages Press, Beijing, China, 2004
Published by Foreign Languages Press
24 Baiwanzhuang Road, Beijing 100037, China
Distributed by China International Book Trading Corporation
35 Chegongzhuang Xilu, Beijing 100044, China
P.O. Box 399, Beijing, China
Printed in the People's Republic of China

Contents

Chapter 1 Economy — 1
1. How Far Away from Modernization Is China? — 2
2. China's Population Experiences an 8 Percent Rate of Economic Growth — 3
3. The Price War in Color TV Sets and Air-conditioners — 6
4. The Position of "Made in China" — 8
5. The Size of the Income Gap — 11
6. Concern for the Private Economy — 15
7. After Entry into the WTO — 17
8. Knowledge Economy Has Made Its Debut — 19
9. When Will the Western Region Become Rich and Prosperous? — 21
10. Status of China's Economy in the World — 24

Chapter 2 Population — 28
1. "Baby Boom" in China — 28
2. China's Population Policy: a Pioneering One — 32
3. The Peasantry: Rapidly Changing into the Working Class — 34
4. Ethnic Minority Population: Now Exceeding 100 Million — 36
5. The General Cultural Quality: Not Good Enough — 38
6. Future Pressures on Providing for the Aged — 40
7. Employment, Employment, and Still Employment — 42
8. An Old Topic of Conversation — 45
9. The Blood-tied Family: Changing into a Marriage-tied Family — 48
10. Future Chinese Population: to Be Less Than 1.55 Billion — 50

Chapter 3 Education   53
1. Education: Enjoying Financial Increments by a Large Margin   54
2. The Heavy Task of Consolidating and Upgrading "the Two Basics"   56
3. From Examination-oriented Education to Quality Education   58
4. Common Folk Benefiting from Enlarged College Enrollment   61
5. A Big Country, Not a Big Power in Higher Education   62
6. A Decade of Rapid Development of Privately-run Education   65
7. What Does Annual Salary of One Million for a Teacher Signify?   67
8. Education for the Disadvantaged Group of People   70
9. IT: Opening up a New Era in Education   73
10. Toward Life-long Learning   75

Chapter 4 Quality of Life   78
1. Huge Increase in Income   78
2. The Scale and Degree of Poverty: Markedly Declined   80
3. The Engel Indicator: Having Declined Dramatically   83
4. Upgrading of the "4 Big Pieces" of Family Possessions   84
5. Consumption of Tourism and Holidays: a New Vogue   86
6. Credit Consumption: Growing Among Urban Families   88
7. Continuing Enthusiasm for Consumption in Health   90
8. Continuous Increase in Consumption of Education   92
9. Social Classifications Beginning to Appear   94
10. Relatively High Degree of Satisfaction Among Urban and Rural Residents   96

Chapter 5 Social Security   98
1. From Unit Security to Social Security   98
2. Great Progress in the Reform of the Social Security System   100

3. Taking Care of the Aged	103
4. The Multi-layer System of Pension Insurance	105
5. The Staggering Reform in the Medical Care Insurance System	107
6. Will the Peak of Unemployment and Laid-off Workers End Safely?	110
7. How to Give Farmers Security?	112
8. Improving the Last Safety Net of Life and Death	115
9. Continuous Development and Improvement of the Social Welfare System	117
10. Difficulties and Prospects for Social Security in China	119

Chapter 6 The Concept of Values and the State of Mind — 122

1. Irresistible Temptations: the Reform and Opening up Program Stirs up the Era of a New State of Mind — 123
2. Collectives vs. Individuals: When Big Rivers Run out of Water, Small Rivers Dry up — 126
3. Paver and Bill: Who Is More Respectable? — 129
4. Post-workplace System: "Iron Rice Bowls" No More — 130
5. Money: How Is It to Be Defined? — 133
6. Love and Marriage: Let Love Dominate — 135
7. Moral Status: Going Forward or Backward? — 137
8. The Internet Era: Facing New Uncertainties — 140
9. High Expectations: Social Development to Which the Chinese People Have Long Looked Forward — 142
10. The Future Trend: Emerging of a New Social Psychology — 144

Chapter 7 Science and Technology — 147

1. Scientific Development Finally Has a System Guarantee — 148
2. Explosive Growth in Scientific and Technological Human Resources — 149
3. Awards Bringing Greater Motive Force — 152
4. Tackling Hard-nut Problems: from Catching up to Overtaking — 154

5. Market: the Key for Scientific and Technological Development	156
6. Space Project: Guarantee for National Security	158
7. China's Contributions to Genetic Projects	161
8. Hybrid Rice Defeating the Threat of Hunger	163
9. Great Benefit from International Exchanges	164
10. Greater International Competitiveness	167

Chapter 8 Environment and Resources   170
1. Awakening of the Awareness of Environmental Protection	171
2. Once Again China Has a Blue Sky	174
3. Longing for Clear Water	177
4. Cleaning Away Garbage Surrounding Urban Areas	180
5. Converting Farmland for Forestry in Action	182
6. Controlling Desertification and Sandstorms	184
7. Protecting Homeless Creatures	187
8. What Are the Treasures?	190
9. In Search of New Energy	192
10. Toward the Blue Ocean	194

Chapter 9 The Reunification of the Country and Unity of the Nation   198
1. "One China": an Inevitable Trend	199
2. Reunification of the Motherland: a Relentless Pursuit	201
3. How Far Away Are the "Three Direct Links"?	203
4. Pearl in the East: Prosperous as Before	206
5. "One Country, Two Systems" Showing Vitality in Macao	208
6. Development of the West: Pushing Forward National Development	210
7. Autonomy in Ethnic Minority Regions: Catching the Attention of the World	213
8. Multicultural Protection, Development and Application	216
9. "Three Non-separations": Increasingly Popular	218
10. The Merits of Overseas Chinese	220

Chapter 10 China and the World   223
  1. Peace: Theme of the Century in Chinese Diplomacy   224
  2. Transcending Ideological Gaps   225
  3. Heads of State Diplomacy: Building a Bridge to the World 228
  4. Successfully Pulling Through the Financial Crisis   230
  5. *Fortune*: China and China's Wealth   233
  6. Win-win for China and the WTO   234
  7. New Concept of Security   236
  8. A Power Engine, Not a Trap in Asia   239
  9. A Big, Responsible Country   241
 10. To Be Wise: Suiting One's Actions to the Times   243

About the Writers   245

Chapter 1 Economy

Since the launching of the reform and opening-up policy at the end of 1978, China has embarked on an economic take-off. The 9.5 average annual growth rate of China's GDP between 1978 and 2000 was three times the average annual increase in the world's economy during the same period, a miracle in the history of the development of world economy. China has now become the sixth largest economic power in the world. For the general population of China, this has meant an end to many long years of shortages. People have experienced profound changes in their daily lives. They no longer have to stand in long lines just to do their shopping, and now sometimes receive discount coupons from businessmen who are promoting sales. The enormous rise in production in China has brought about the brisk sales of Chinese products worldwide. "Made in China" products can be found everywhere in Europe, America, Japan, and many other developed countries, and some of these commodities have become daily necessities. The colossal and rapid growth of the economy and the rich supply of good quality products at low prices have given full expression to China's influence in the world.

During the process of rapid development, China has accumulated rich experiences and lessons, but at the same time China also faces new challenges and opportunities.

1. How Far Away from Modernization Is China?

Modernization is a term that is often spoken of and discussed in detail in China, and its theoretical principles have been established through long-term practice. However, reaching the actual modernization standard is a much more complicated affair, and to this day there is still no final agreement as to how or when it will be fully reached.

After World War II, some economists began to explore index systems for measuring the degree of modernization, and internationally there are now many institutions and scholars that use such a set of socio-economic indexes to measure the level of modernization. The most representative of these is one American sociologist who has set forth 10 indexes to measure the level of modernization: the per-capita GDP (gross domestic product), the proportion of agricultural output value in the GNP (gross national product), etc.

Chinese scholars have also paid much attention to and carried out long-term studies of modernization. They have put forward a variety of index systems and methods and they have made appropriate estimates.

In 2000, Prof. Zhu Qingfang, a scholar with the Chinese Academy of Social Sciences (CASS), appraised China's modernization level using the American sociologist's standards and came to the conclusion that China's modernization was 81.9 percent of those standards in 1998, ranking it 66th in the world. He estimated that, in accordance with the development rate of the past 20 years since the start of the reform and opening-up program, China should be able to reach the modernization standard in 13 years.

In its "2001 Report on China's Sustainable Development Strategy," the Chinese Academy of Sciences (CAS) Sustainable Development Research Group stated that China would still have to speed up its economic pace by nearly 60 percentage points to reach a level of 0.404 (i.e., 40.4 percent), the level of moderately developed countries in today's world. They said that China would reach the level of moderately developed countries and realize modernization in the year 2050.

In 2002, the "China Modernization Strategy Studies" research report, a study supported by the Ministry of Science and Technology, the Chinese Academy of Sciences, and the State Natural Science Fund Committee, stated: China has entered the first modernization development period. The level of China's first modernization was 76 percent in 2000. The modernization process has two major stages: The first takes the development of the industrial economy as its basic characteristic; the second takes the development of a knowledge-oriented economy as its basic characteristic. By 1999 there were 61 countries in the world that had completed, or basically completed, the first modernization; and 29 countries, including the United States, had embarked on the track of second modernization; while 37 countries, including China, were in the development period of the first modernization.

2. China's Population Experiences an 8 Percent Rate of Economic Growth

An 8 percent rate of economic growth refers to 8 percent growth in the GDP (gross domestic product). The GDP is a monetary expression covering the final products produced by a country or a region within a certain period of time and the aggregate of the labor service this provides. In the words of the noted economist Paul Anthony Samuelson, this means the market value of service and all products ranging from apples to zithers produced in one year.

The GDP has increasingly become one of the most common economic concepts in measuring the daily life of people. GDP is the term used in the World Bank's annual "World Development Report." The index of China's GDP first appeared in China's "Government Work Report" in 2002. This said that the 2001 GDP grew by 7.3 percent over the previous year. Even microeconomic activities such as enterprise investment and residents' purchases of houses and cars are inseparable from the analysis of the GDP. This most important index in economics reflects, as a whole, the general scale of economic activity, overall economic strength, and level of the people's living standards in a country or a region.

The deepest and most direct impression gained by people as a result of a rapid growth in the GDP is the enhancement of national strength and the rise in living standards. Over the past 20-odd years since the initiation of the reform and opening up program, the average annual growth rate of China's GDP was 9.5 percent, making it the country with the fastest economic growth in the world. This high-speed rise in the GDP has brought about a leapfrog development for China's productive forces, outstripping Italy, whose economy was 2.3 times China's economic aggregate just twenty years ago. This has made China the world's 6th economic power in the world. The output of China's main industrial and agricultural products was all in the front ranks. "Made in China" products are selling well in the international market, and Chinese citizens have experienced fundamental changes in their daily lives, saying farewell to the era of shortages. There is a great variety of commodities in the marketplace, and people are generally well-off.

What does an 8 percent growth rate imply? What is an 8 percent growth rate and can 8 percent be realized? These are not only matters of concern to ordinary people, but they are questions that need to be studied and answered by economists as well. From the perspective of quantitative relations, if the GDP grows at the rate of 8 percent annually on average, then it can increase to twice its size in as much as nine years' time, that is to say, an 8 percent economic growth rate implies a doubling of the GDP in ten years.

In March 1998, the newly elected premier of the State Council, Zhu Rongji, summarized the main items of work of the government in that term as "one guarantee, three things put in place, and five reforms." One guarantee meant that China's GDP was assured of an 8 percent growth in 1998. This was required by the new situation facing economic development at the turn of the century. Because of the Asian financial crisis and the slow growth of the world economy, China's export level slowed down. The international situation was grim, and the domestic demand was inadequate. Enterprises suffered losses or had difficulties in operation, the growth of residents' incomes was slow, employment pressures were mounting — these socio-economic problems had to be resolved through a rapid growth in the GDP. It is the view of experts that China's present employment elasticity stands at around 0.1. With every 1 percent of GDP growth, it can add 700,000-1,000,000 job opportunities. The grim employment situation can be greatly alleviated only by keeping the GDP at an 8 percent growth rate.

It is possible to maintain an 8 percent growth rate in the GDP. However the growth rate in the GDP is not unrestrained. It is subject to the restriction of technical and economic conditions. Under the condition of established technology and population size, as well as controls to prevent accelerated inflation, the government has called for the maintenance of the highest GDP level as the potential GDP. According to expert analysis, China's potential GDP growth rate stands at above 8 percent. Therefore, setting the GDP growth rate at 8 percent has its theoretical and practical foundations.

An 8 percent GDP growth rate is the requirement for achieving Deng Xiaoping's three-step strategic goal. China had, by 1995, realized the first two-step strategic goal for its modernization drive ahead of schedule: the quadrupling of its 1980 GDP by the end of the 20th century through an average annual growth rate of approximately 7.3 percent GDP between 1980 and 1995. China has now begun to implement the third-step strategic plan, and it will basically realize modernization by the middle of this century. The Tenth Five-year Plan (2001-05) clearly states that maintaining a relatively fast development rate in the national economy has laid a solid foundation for a doubling of the 2000 GDP by the year 2010. Since the average annual growth rate for doubling the GDP in ten years stands at 7.2 percent, it is thus clear that an 8 percent growth rate in the GDP is a basic guarantee for the achievement of national modernization.

3. The Price War in Color TV Sets and Air-conditioners

In recent years a price war has been raging in the Chinese markets. Consumers are beginning to believe that there is nothing in limited supply in the market and that the prices of all commodities are falling. For enterprises the striking feeling is that whatever is produced is piling up and it is increasingly difficult to market products. Such a phenomenon points to the arrival of an excess economy and the emergence of a buyer's market, and the matter is being widely debated among economists.

The fact that the epoch of shortages is now gone is one of the most noticeable and most important changes to take place in China's economy during the past twenty years of reform and opening up efforts. Everyone clearly remembers the practice of lining up for shopping, and that just a dozen years or so ago almost all commodities were supplied against coupons. It is almost unbelievable that the shortage of commodities has disappeared in only the short space of twenty years. The emergence of such a buyer's market marks a major change in the supply and demand relations of the market. It is an extremely important milestone in marking the fundamental changes in people's lives, and the profound alteration in the scale of the market economy.

An important reason for this excess of goods in the market is overproduction. As far as the Chinese people are concerned, another reason for the excess is the existence of obstacles to change in the higher-level consumption patterns. At the end of the last century, any rise in the residents' consumption levels was manifest mainly in changes in the variety and grade of durable consumer goods, with a continuing popularization of the consumption of 1,000-yuan and 10,000-yuan-class durable articles, such as television sets, refrigerators, air-conditioners, handsets, and computers. Now the further upgrading in the consumption level has met with obstructions. This is because first, it is still impossible for the income levels of ordinary families, through their own accumulations, to rise to a consumption stage that allows for the normal purchase of 10,000-yuan-class commodities, such as automobiles and houses. Second, it is the fact that residents' incomes are increasingly becoming separated by economic status, with the consumption of the high-income stratum tending to reach a saturated state, while the low-income stratum is limited to the consumption of basic necessities. All these factors have lowered the consumption level. At the same time, housing, medical costs, and education needs have raised people's anticipated expenditures and lowered their immediate consumption. This is one of the reasons why residents' savings deposits continue to grow despite a successive lowering of interest rates.

There are both supply and demand reasons and institutional factors for the emergence of an excess economy. Both the government and the enterprises are faced with the question of how to transform these mechanisms.

This kind of excess economy emerged under the circumstance of a relatively low level of economic development, China's per capita GDP is only US $800, or equivalent to just 16 percent of the world's average. The per capita electricity consumption in China is equivalent to only 35 percent of the world's average. Therefore excess, even when it exists, is a relative excess and a structural excess. The academic community has different views on whether or not "an excess economy has arrived" in China.

4. The Position of "Made in China"

With the brisk sales of large amounts of Chinese products in the international market, many of which are the daily necessities of people, such as clothing, food, housing, and transportation, the topic of "Made in China" has become an area of great concern to many people. International opinion holds that the world's manufacturing center is shifting toward China and that the world has entered into a "Made-in-China age." Japan's *Sankei Shimbun* has published a series of articles saying that "China has become a world factory in terms of its manufacturing industry." An article published in a newspaper of the Republic of Korea (ROK) holds that China has replaced Korea in becoming a regional power in terms of industrial manufacture for the international market. One out of every two air-conditioners now comes from China. Its television sets and washing machines make up one-third and one-fourth respectively of international sales. By 2010, China will surpass ROK in all the important industrial fields.

It is an indisputable fact that China is becoming the manufacturing base for certain products. China's manufacturing industry has built up to a sizeable scale, ranking it fourth in the world. The State Economic and Trade Commission indicated in April 2002 that China had become the world's main manufacturing base for household electrical appliances. The output of many of these home appliances is in the front ranks of the world. For example, the output of air-conditioners has exceeded 23 million; micro-wave stoves 18.18 million; washing machines 13.34 million, and refrigerators 13.49 million.

Dongguan, in China's southern Guangdong Province, has become an important base for the world computer manufacturing industry. Its computer information products have a considerable share of the global market. Its semi-conductor parts of computer magnetic heads and computer chassis have a 40 percent share, copper clad panels and computer drivers

30 percent, advanced alternate capacitors and output transformers 25 percent, computer scanners and micro motors 20 percent, and main computer boards 15 percent. It is said that over 95 percent of parts and components needed for the manufacture of complete computers can be obtained in Dongguan.

According to a survey conducted by the Japanese Ministry of Industrial Economy, China's motorcycles represent 43 percent of the world output, computer keyboards 39 percent, household air-conditioners 32 percent, washing machines 26 percent, color TV sets 23 percent, chemical fibers 21 percent, and refrigerators 19 percent. At the same time, regions represented by the Pearl River Delta and the Yangtze River Delta have become important bases for handling the outward shift of the world's manufacturing industry, receiving a large share of the manufacturing industry from the regions of Hong Kong, Taiwan, Japan, and ROK, as well as Europe and North America. At the beginning of this century, the manufacturing links of transnational corporations began a new round of shifts toward China. The globe's second largest electronics manufacturing service, Ericsson, declared that it would shift its production, outer packing, and order forms on most cell phones to China within two years. At much the same time, Motorola disclosed that it would increase investments to enormously expand its Asian communication production base in Tianjin.

However, behind the prosperous "Made in China" scene is a grim fact that the lack of core technology has created a soreness that is impossible to dispel from the hearts of the Chinese. In the transferred industries thus undertaken, equipment, technology and markets are still basically held in the hands of foreign capital. What China provides is mainly cheap land, cheap labor, and a huge market. China's original national industries operate at a low technological level and lack innovative capability and market competitiveness. Generally speaking, China mainly relies on imports for its industrial technology, relying on the import of most of the equipment needed for the national economy and high-tech industries. Over the past few years of fixed asset investments in the whole society, two-thirds of the equipment investments have had to rely on imports, while 100 percent of the optical fiber manufacturing equipment, 85 percent of the integrated circuit chips manufacturing equipment, 80 percent of the petro-chemical equipment, and 70 percent of the automobile manufacturing equipment, numerical-control machine tools, textile machinery, and offset equipment are occupied by imported products. This is a fundamental reason why personages concerned are loudly crying out for rejuvenating China's manufacturing industry. China is faced with a severe challenge as to how it can really become the world's manufacturing base, and not be a production or processing center.

5. The Size of the Income Gap

Along with the rapid economic development since the launch of the reform and opening up policy, Chinese residents' incomes and living standards have been raised enormously. The average per capita income for urban residents has increased 18-fold from 344 yuan in 1978 to 6,280 yuan in 2000, and that of rural dwellers grew 17-fold from 134 yuan to 2,253 yuan in the same period. Calculated on the basis of comparable prices, the figures were 4.77-fold and 3.49-fold respectively in the year concerned. The degree of people's affluence kept rising, the quality of residents' life went up steadily, and the consumption pattern was improved gradually. The Engel's coefficient of urban and rural dwellers stood at 41.9 percent and 52.6 percent respectively in 1999; and per capita housing for urban and rural residents has reached 9.8 square meters and 24.4 square meters respectively. Automobiles have begun to be purchased in significant quantities by urban families, with 3.4 households out of every one thousand possessing private cars. Also motorcycles have assumed the trend of popularization among rural households where 165 motorcycles are now owned by every 1,000 households.

As for communications, the dream of "knowing world affairs without going out" has been achieved. The number of the nation's fixed telephone users has reached 110 million households, mobile phone users 43.3 million households, and Internet users 3 million households. As for household appliances, wide-screen, high-clarity color television sets and modern, large capacity and multi-door refrigerators have become urban residents' objective in updating their home necessities. Color TVs, refrigerators, and washing machines are also more and more entering into the homes of farm families. People are generally experiencing a relatively comfortable life.

The rise in income levels has been accompanied by a growth in the income gap. The widening of China's income disparity has become one of the major issues of common concern to society. The Gin coefficient is the most commonly used method for describing the gap between the rich and poor. The Gin coefficient generally lies between 0 and 1. When the coefficient is 0, this indicates that the income distribution is absolutely equal. When it is 1, this indicates that the income distribution is far from equal. It is generally held that a Gin coefficient of less than 0.2 is highly equal, and if larger than 0.6, highly unequal. Internationally, 0.4 is usually regarded as a warning line. Many Chinese experts and scholars have respectively made estimates of the Gin coefficient and the numerical values they have obtained are different. But most experts hold that before the introduction of the reform and opening up program, China's income distribution was in a highly equal state with a Gin coefficient smaller than 0.2. Since the start of the reform and opening up program, the continual expansion of the Chinese income gap has been a publicly acknowledged fact. Now China's Gin coefficient is larger than 0.4 and it has surpassed the international warning line. This is identical with the personal experience of the common people in their daily lives.

The reasons for the generation of this disparity in the Chinese residents' income distribution is mainly due to the fact that the highly centralized traditional planned economy and the mono-system of public ownership has been broken down by the reform of the economic system. The result has given rise to contradictions between the new and old systems that have produced loopholes in the process of restructuring and has been hindered by the monopolies of the trades; state investment, taxation and other policies; differences in enterprise operation, and various kinds of illegal action.

In studies on income distribution, the inverted U-shaped theoretical hypothesis set forth by noted American economist, Simon Kutznets, holds a primary position in traditional economic theory. This presumption says that along with per capita GDP growth in the process of economic development, the locus of long-term change in the disparity of income distribution is an inverted U-shaped curve, i.e., economic growth will gradually expand in the initial period and gradually shrink in the later stage. The theory on early development maintains that an expansion of the income gap in the process of economic growth is unavoidable and can improve economic efficiency. The problem of income disparity can be resolved only through economic growth, and therefore exponents of this theory advocate that fairness should be realized only after economic growth. Since the 1980s, people have gained an ever-deeper understanding of the fairness and efficiency relationship, and they have paid more attention to the negative effects resulting from the unequal distribution of incomes. They believe that the unequal distribution will lead to a dampening of work enthusiasm, a reduction in work efficiency; inequality in development opportunities, and it will affect the low-income earners' ability to contribute toward the national economy. It will create a domestic political-economic environment filled with uncertainties, affect the investor's confidence, and finally hamper the realization of economic growth. Therefore, they advocate achieving growth through fairness.

Since the start of the reform and opening up program, China has adopted the economic development strategy of "putting efficiency first, while giving due consideration to fairness." The phenomenal achievements gained in China's economy fully prove that this is a correct road for the advance from universal poverty to general prosperity. But the existing problem of the gap between the poor and the rich has become a question which the Chinese people are most concerned about in their daily lives. The state is adopting effective measures, including cleaning-up and rectifying the income distribution system, the transfer of financial payments, stepping up the establishment and perfection of the social security system, the large-scale development of the western region, and striving to properly solve the fairness and efficiency relations in economic development so as to ensure the sustained and rapid development of the national economy and the continued elevation of people's living standards.

6. Concern for the Private Economy

China's private economy began from a zero starting-point in the early 1980s and grew up slowly within limited segments of the traditional system and far removed from the mainstream of society. The private economy blazed an arduous and tortuous road. In 1987, after the start of the reform and opening up endeavor, the CPC Central Committee's Decision "On Guiding Rural Reform Toward In-depth Development" stated for the first time that private enterprises were to be allowed to exist. The "Amendment to the Constitution of the People's Republic of China" explicitly set forth the concept of a "private economy," and established it as a "supplement to the socialist public economy," thus giving private economy a legal status. In 1997 the CPC 15th National Congress lifted the non-public economies from a supplementary status to the status of being an important component part of the socialist market economy. As a result, the private economy and other non-state-run economies gained a social status equal to that of the public economy.

In the short 15-year period of time, the achievements scored by the private economy are gratifying and amazing. Statistics show that by 1999, the number of investors for private enterprises registered nationwide had approached 3 million; the total amount of registered capital they possessed came to 1028.7 billion yuan; they had 20.22 million employees, and they operated around 1.509 million enterprises of various types. Between 1990 and 1999, the number of private enterprises jumped from 98,000 to 1.509 million, a 16.4-fold increase. Their average annual rate of growth was 35.5 percent, much higher than that for the state-owned, collective, or foreign-invested enterprises. The registered capital of private enterprises shot up from 950 million yuan to 1028.7 billion yuan, with an average annual growth of 68.2 percent, respectively four-fold, six-fold and two-fold the growth rates of state-owned, collective, and foreign-funded enterprises during the same period. The business scale of the private enterprises witnessed constant expansion; per-enterprise registered capital grew from 96,800 yuan to 681,000 yuan, a 37.04-fold increase, with an average annual growth rate of 24.22 percent. In the same period the registered capital per-enterprise of state-owned, collective and foreign-funded enterprises increased 2.55-fold, 2.58-fold and 1.68-fold respectively. By 1990, the registered funds per private enterprise respectively were 9.3 percent, 60.1 percent, and 7.4 percent in comparison to those of the state-owned, collective and foreign-invested enterprises. And by 1999, the figures respectively reached 25.9 percent, 164.3 percent, and 31.2 percent.

Private enterprises have not only witnessed constant expansion of their business scale, but their contribution to the national economy and their social-economic influence have also been on the increase. Between 1990 and 1999, the output value achieved by private enterprises increased from 12.2 billion yuan to 768.6 billion yuan, with average annual growth rate of 49.08 percent calculated on the basis of comparable prices. Their proportion to the nation's industrial and commercial tax revenue increased from 0.06 percent to 2.48 percent. In 1999, there were 20.22 million employees in private enterprises. Their proportion to all personnel of society went up from 0.3 percent in 1989 to 2.86 percent in 1999. At present, about half of the unemployed workers in various localities have entered individual and private enterprises, thus greatly alleviating the pressure of employment on the country and making a contribution to maintaining social stability.

Private enterprises boast clear property rights and sound mechanisms, and they have very strong vitality in the increasingly intense market competition. At present, besides being restricted by the macro-environment and the political system, private enterprises face the following problems: their scale is small, name brands are few, investment fields are narrow, and the quality and managerial level of the operators are in urgent need of improvement. These problems have caught the attention of the government and public enterprises, and the private enterprises are growing up amidst greater challenges and opportunities.

7. After Entry into the WTO

In 2002, the China Economic Boom Monitoring Center, together with the China Finance-Economy Report program of the China Central TV, conducted a questionnaire as to the quality of life, ideological concepts, and employment levels within five years after China's accession to the World Trade Organization (WTO). They interviewed more than 600 persons during the survey. A total of 59.6 percent of those interviewed predicted that in the coming five years the quality of life would be much better than what it was at the time of interview. From this favorable anticipation of life as reported by most of the respondents, it can be seen that people have confidence in China's economy during the crucial five years after China's accession to the WTO. They believe that as China integrates into the world in an all-round way, they are bound to benefit from the rise in the country's economic level. At the same time, 38.5 percent of the residents estimated that the quality of life for themselves and their families would be equal to what it was at the time of interview, holding that greater development was yet to come, only 2 percent predicted that life would barely be satisfactory. With regard to the social service level, 91.5 percent of the residents estimated that there would be a rise in the general service level of society in the coming five years. The competitive situation in the gradually formed modern service trades has cheered up the overwhelming majority of people. People expect that there will be more and better choices, and that service up to international standards will be found everywhere in China in the future.

The fact that China formally joined the WTO in November 2001 shows that China will participate in world competition and cooperation on a wider scope, will enjoy the fruits of multilateral negotiation, and obtain the opportunity to enter the markets of other countries. From a long-term point of view, this participation will generate a positive influence on China's economic growth and its foreign trade, and it will bring numerous business opportunities for the growth of China's traditional labor-intensive products and technology and for the export of its light industrial products which have reached a definite scale. The World Bank has estimated that five years after China's accession to the WTO, the proportion of the country's trade volume in the world will increase from the present 4.5 percent to 6.5 percent.

Since the WTO entry, Chinese enterprises face the fierce competition of foreign enterprises, and the situation of China's economic development mainly depends on the status and strength of Chinese enterprises in this international contest. There are still many defects in China's current economic system that has made it more difficult for the Chinese enterprises that lack international competitiveness to meet the challenge posed by international competition.

But this can be beneficial, not harmful, to the Chinese people. With an increase in the total volume of employment and alteration in the employment structure, the situation characterized by "externally low and internally high" and "externally high and internally low" prices for domestic commodities will undergo changes. Chinese consumers should experience more consumption choices and cheaper commodities.

Since joining the WTO, Chinese state-owned enterprises and national banks face an outstanding problem, i.e., the shortage of professionals. Therefore, one of the main tasks for Chinese higher education is to train various types of professionals as soon as possible. Particularly, legal personnel are urgently needed in the establishment of a socialist market that is opening up to the outside world.

8. Knowledge Economy Has Made Its Debut

The power and value of knowledge has become increasingly evident in China. People should remember that soon after the start of reform and opening up in late 1978, some people, in the face of the situation of an unfair social distribution between mental and manual labor, sighed and said that "Creating atomic bombs is not as good as selling preserved eggs; holding a surgeon's scalpel is not as good as holding a barber's razor." Now there are few such statements because, along with the socio-economic development and the increasing role played by the market mechanisms, people with genuine knowledge and creative abilities are being given due respect and put into important positions in society.

As humanity marched toward the 21st century, there was a marked tendency in world economic development for knowledge to become increasingly tangible and scientific. Technological progress increasingly resulted in strength in economic development. This period was also a time for the global trial of knowledge. Fritz Machlup, an American economist, put forward the important concept of the knowledge industry as early as the 1950s. Since the mid-20th century, the development of high technology has provided an objective environment for the formation and development of the knowledge industry. An important field in the knowledge industry, as defined by Machlup, is the information industry and its directly related industries.

In recent years, the world information industry has developed rapidly. The enterprises directly related to the information industry, which entered the ranks of the world's top 500 businesses, have occupied an important position among the world's top 500 businesses both in terms of business scale and in terms of the total amount of profits. They have become a pillar industry in economic development in the world. Among the world's top 500 enterprises in the year 2000, the business volume of communications, electronic and electrical equipment industries, computer and office apparatus industries, computer service and software industries, network communication industries, and publishing and printing industries reached US $2057.2 billion, a 13.7 percent increase over the previous year, accounting for 14.6 percent of the total business volume of the top 500 businesses. Their profit volume hit US $122.3 billion, up 5.7 percent year-on-year, which represented 18.3 percent of the gross profit volume of these top 500 businesses, demonstrating the strong vitality of the information industry in its development.

Judging from the process of the development of the knowledge-based economy in developed countries, entrepreneurs proficient in science and technology have the most ideal talents for the development of the knowledge economy. Because these entrepreneurs generally have a strong grounding in science and technology commodities and can use their own background knowledge in natural science and engineering technology to engage in the development, production, and operational activities in the high-tech field. They can identify and grasp the technological and market trends more easily than ordinary entrepreneurs. Thus the products they develop have greater competitiveness. In addition, hi-tech enterprises are also knowledge-intensive enterprises. Therefore, the legal persons in these enterprises generally have extensive natural science and technology engineering knowledge, or they have scored outstanding achievements in these fields. The personnel they lead are also mostly professionals with hi-tech knowledge.

9. When Will the Western Region Become Rich and Prosperous?

After mobilizing public opinion and conducting feasibility studies of the development plans over the past two years, substantive steps have been taken in the large-scale development of the western region, especially with the powerful support of favorable state policies and national treasury funds. Many construction projects, such as west-to-east natural gas transfer, west-to-east electricity transmission, and the construction of the Qinghai-Tibet Railway have been started. Project construction related to the comprehensive improvement of the ecological environment has been launched in an all-around way. At present, infrastructure construction is surging forward in the vast expanse of the western region. During the year 2001, the investment growth rate in the central region was higher than that in the eastern region by 3 percentage points, while that in the western region was also higher than the central region by 3 percentage points.

The landmass of west China accounts for 57 percent of the national total and its population for 23 percent of the national total. But in 1999, that region's GDP represented only 14 percent of the national total. The per capita GDP was 4,250 yuan, equivalent to only about 60 percent of the national average, and less than 47 percent of the per capita value of the eastern region. The per capita disposable income of urban residents and the net income of farmers in the western region in that year were 5,058 yuan and 1,583 yuan respectively, equivalent to only 86 percent and 72 percent of the nation's same indexes, and only one-half and one-third of the same indexes for the eastern region. The total volume of retail sales in social commodities in the western region in that year made up only 13 percent of the national total, and the region's per-capita purchasing power was only 47 percent of the national average. Over one half of the country's poverty-stricken counties were concentrated in the western region, and 90 percent of the country's poorest population was concentrated in the western region. In the twenty years since the start of the reform and opening up, the economic growth rate of the western region was 1.1 percent lower than the national average, and 4.1 percent lower than that of the eastern region. With such a disparity, no wonder the people of the western region questioned "whether we still belong to China."

In the main "hot spot" countries of today's world, there are many reasons for political turbulence and civil wars. These include tribal contradictions and religious conflicts, but fundamentally the focus of the issue lies in the excessive income and development gaps between various population groups and between regions.

The potential advantages of the western region are manifest in terms of its resources — energy, mineral, and biological resources. Also the potential advantages of the western region are manifest in its beautiful natural landscape, strong ethnic customs and conditions, and rich historical and cultural accretions, all of which are valuable tourist resources. The western region also boasts first-rate domestic universities and scientific research institutes. Shaanxi Province alone has more than 40 institutions of higher learning and over 2,000 scientific research institutes of various kinds. Its overall science and technology strength ranks third in the country. The obstacles facing the western region in their development include: backward ideological concepts, a worsening ecological environment, obsolete infrastructure facilities, an unfavorable institutional and market environment, low industrial level, fast population growth, poor labor quality, insufficient innovative capabilities in science and technology, low level of opening to the outside world, and limited outward driving force.

To carry out large-scale development of the western region, it will be necessary not only to pay attention to education and training of local personnel, but also to successfully introduce non-local talent. As to the policy for introducing personnel, it is both necessary to increase the attraction of wages and allowances, and to create an environment in which personnel may come and go freely. The past practice of "dedicating one's youth and then one's son and grandson" must not be repeated. The factor of labor cost must be taken into full consideration when starting projects. Only in this way can the bottleneck of human resources that restrict large-scale development of the western region be really alleviated.

10. Status of China's Economy in the World

Between 1978 and 2000, the average annual growth of China's GDP was 9.5 percent, making China the country with the fastest growth rate in the world. This speed was three times the average annual growth rate of the rest of the world economy during the same period, creating a miracle in the development history of the world economy. The high-speed economic growth has resulted in the enormous rise in the level of China's productive forces and national strength. China has surpassed Italy to become the world's sixth economic power, whereas twenty years ago Italy was much stronger than China, with the former's GDP being 2.3 times that of the latter. Twenty years ago, the economic aggregates of China, Mexico, Spain, India, the Netherlands, Australia and other countries were approximately the same, but today

China's economic aggregate is respectively 2.5-fold, 1.6-fold, 2.3-fold, 2.3-fold and 2.1-fold greater than theirs. Only two decades ago, China's GDP was 1.87 percent of the world's total, today the figure is 3.28 percent. Then, China made up just 7.45 percent of the GDP of the United States, the number one power in the world. Today the figure has risen to 11.38 percent. In twenty years' time, the world's GDP increased 2.8-fold, while China's economic aggregate made a miraculous growth of 4.9-fold!

The output for the overwhelming majority of China's important industrial and agricultural products has jumped to the front ranks of the world. Of the main agricultural products, the output of cereals, meat, cotton, peanuts, rapeseed, fruit, and other products all rank first in the world! The output of its tea, soybeans, and sugarcane ranks third. Among the principal industrial products, the output of steel, coal, cement, chemical fertilizers, and television sets all rank first in the world, while power output, cotton cloth, and chemical fibers rank second, and its sugar ranks fourth, crude oil ranks fifth, and there has been a remarkable elevation in the ranking of other products.

China's miracle has shaken the world and attracted world attention. In his new work *World Economy: Past and Future*, the well-known American economist, Walt Whitman Rostow, made the following observation: Of Asia as a late-comer in modernization as a whole, Japan has flown to the sky in the first flight; the "four small Asian dragons" — Hong Kong, Taiwan, Singapore, and South Korea followed closely on its heels in the second flight; China has started on the new flight of the 21st century. It will open up new air routes and will fly into the sky. Former US National Security Adviser Zbigniew Brzezinski holds that China will be the next giant on the world stage.

Many people predict that China will be able to catch up with the world's number one power — the United States — to become the world's new number one power. According to Angus Maddison, calculated on the basis of the PPP (purchasing power parity) in 1998, in 1987 China's GDP was equivalent to 23 percent of that of the United States; the figure rose to 52 percent in 1995 and 60.6 percent in 2000, and can be expected to surpass the United States by around 2015. Former prime minister of Singapore, Lee Kuan Yew, held that the scale of China's economy could reach US $2 trillion in fifty years, the equivalent to around four-fifths that of the United States. Many people at home also have made simple mathematical computations by assuming that the present aggregate and speed should be taken as a precondition. Thus, since the GDP of China and the United States stand respectively at US $1 trillion and US $9 trillion, with the growth rates being 8 percent and 3 percent respectively, then China's GDP will catch up and overtake that of the United States in about 47 years. In the view of the World Bank, China's GDP is US $4 trillion based on the PPP, while a report of the US National Security Council held that China's GDP has reached US $6 trillion. Calculated on this basis, China's GDP would surpass that of the United States in twenty years.

In 1996, when studying the "analysis of China's economic development at various stages and the choice of pillar industries by 2050," scholars of the Chinese Academy of Social Sciences also made a comparative analysis of Chinese and US economic scales. While comparing the prospects for the two countries' economic development, they said that economic growth, inflation, and exchange rates would commonly play roles. Through studies it was discovered that in the 1964-93 period, the economic growth rates of Japan and Singapore were not only higher than those of the United States, but were also accompanied by substantial monetary values added. Their exchange rates rose by 300 percent and 200 percent respectively. This can be regarded as the secret of the rapid expansion of the economic aggregate of these two countries. The conclusion drawn from the research at that time was: China's GDP would surpass that of the United States in 2030, making it the country with the largest economic aggregate in the world by that time, and it would be two times that of the United States in 2050.

These different conclusions on the future development of China's economic scale should not affect the sober understanding of China's present development stage, from the perspective of per capita GDP — a key index in measuring the development level of a country. China's GDP is still at a very low level. In 1999, China's per capita GDP was only US $780, placing it the 140th in the world, representing 40 percent of the average of the world's medium-income countries, 16 percent of the world's average level, 3 percent of the average level of high-income countries, and 2.5 percent of that of the United States. At the same time, China's urbanization level was only 36 percent, while the employed population stood as high as 50 percent in agricultural areas. These figures indicate that China had just entered the ranks of the medium- and low-income countries. The road is long and the task arduous for China to realize modernization.

(Written by Li Ping)

Chapter 2   Population

The rumbling train loaded with Chinese people meandered through the open country of 20th century China. Whenever the train passed through another year, there were new passengers added, 20 million in number. However, the train did not slow down due to overloading because the history of the entire 20th century revealed that the length of the train was continually extending in China, the world's most populous country. Its pull and speed were also on the increase, even in the last twenty years of the 20th century. This speeding train brought the attention of other members of the Global Village to the unprecedented growth rate in China.

But we must not be complacent, because the pressure of the total volume of the population has become increasingly weighty.

During the first forty years of the 21st century, when the growth of Chinese population reaches its peak, there will be two major issues facing the nation: great employment pressures in the first twenty years and the heavy burden of providing for the aged in the last twenty years.

1. "Baby Boom" in China

The term "baby boom" is used by demographers to describe population growth after World War II. Postwar marriages and child-bearing have led to the birth of huge numbers of children within a short space of time, giving rise to the so-called baby boom.

China's "baby boom," when compared with that of Western countries, is somewhat like a small sorcerer in the presence of a great one. The total amount of China's population in the past was not known because there was no strict census before the founding of the People's Republic of China in 1949. Even the leading authorities at that time did not know the exact number of Chinese people. Yet certain academic members of the elite and some political leaders were deeply worried about the limited amount of Chinese population. For example, both Liang Qichao (1873-1929), a bourgeois reformist and scholar of modern China, and Sun Yat-sen, who led the Revolution of 1911 to overthrow the last feudal dynasty of the Qing, were so concerned.

Although the two were as incompatible as fire and water in their political views, they were surprisingly in agreement in their understanding of the size of Chinese population under the circumstances of the invasion of China by foreign powers. Both were exponents of the theory of an insufficient population, and both encouraged population growth to prevent national subjugation and genocide. According to Dr. Sun, the gross population of 400 million Chinese had continued for as long as 200 years. This view even affected certain principal Chinese Party and government leaders at that time. In September 1949, in his opening address at the First Session of the Chinese People's Political Consultative Conference (CPPCC), Chairman Mao Zedong said that the total number of the Chinese people had reached 475 million.

But the first census China conducted on July 1, 1953 revealed that the gross Chinese population that year topped 594 million. The disparity of these two figures — 594 million and 475 million — was 119 million. When the net population growth in the three years of 1950, 1951, and 1952 was estimated to be 40 million (average annual net increase of around 13 million), then the gross population on the Chinese mainland in 1949 should have stood at around 550 million. It can thus be seen that the wrong population figure provided by the scholars to Chairman Mao in 1949 put the error at around 80 million.

In peacetime, at the rapid growth of population, people first shout and jump for joy, and then become tongue-tied. In his *New Theory of Population,* Mr. Ma Yinchu said, "Now the general estimate is that Chinese mainland's population probably increases by 12-13 million annually, with a growth rate of 20 per thousand," but, "I think the population growth rate in the past four years possibly stood at above 20 per thousand." Deng Xiaoping, then vice premier of the Government Administration Council, predecessor of today's State Council, repeatedly called for controlling the population volume after the release of the data obtained from the first national census. Unfortunately, Mr. Ma Yinchu's *New Theory of Population* was later subjected to mistaken criticism, and the country failed to adopt a timely family planning policy.

Influenced by the "baby boom" elsewhere, there was strong momentum for a rapid growth in the Chinese population. During the nine years between 1950 and 1958, the number of China's annual newborns reached an average of around 20 million thanks to social stability, economic growth, and employment increases. Although there was a slight reduction in the three difficult years of 1959, 1960 and 1961, the number of newborns stood at 16.47 million, 13.89 million and 11.88 million respectively. But in the ten years from 1962 to 1972, China's annual newborns stood at almost more than 25 million. The figure even hit 29.54 million in 1968. This was equivalent to the combined total of the populations of Taiwan and Hong Kong in 2000. When the government realized the tremendous pressures exerted by this population growth on the development of the national economy, they began to vigorously implement a family planning policy in the 1970s. As a result, there appeared a trend toward the decline in the natural population growth, which fell from over 25 per thousand in the 1960s to about 12 per thousand in the 1970s.

In the early 1980s, due to various reasons, there was a pick-up in the natural growth rate of Chinese population, hovering between 13 per thousand and 16 per thousand. But for the entire period of the 1990s, national leaders had a firmer understanding of this development than at any time before. In March each year, General Secretary Jiang Zemin emphasized the importance of controlling the amount and improving the quality of life for the population at the central working forum on the environment of population resources. This has entailed a steady decline in the natural growth rate of China's population. It had finally dropped to 9.35 per thousand in 1998 and further to 8.77 per thousand in 1999.

Implementation of the family planning policy brought the growth rate of the Chinese population under effective control. If the figure of natural growth was estimated to be around 10 million in 2001, then, on the basis of 1.265 billion in 2000, the total population should be at around 1.276 billion at the end of 2001.

2. China's Population Policy: a Pioneering One

The ratio between the birth rate and the death rate of a population determines the natural growth rate. If the birth rate outdoes the mortality rate, then there is a net growth in the population; if the death rate outstrips the birth rate, then there is a net reduction in the population. It can be seen from existing data that the death rate of China's population was reduced to below 10 per thousand after the founding of the People's Republic in 1949. If China's population was at the stage of a high birth rate, high death rate, and low natural growth rate before 1949, then China's population afterward turned into the stage of a high birth rate, low mortality rate, and high natural growth rate due to social stability and production development. The growth rate of the urban population in the early period of the People's Republic remained high for a long time, standing at 36.01 per thousand in 1957. But in the 1960s, due to the establishment of a rural cooperative medical and health system, the death rate of the rural population swiftly declined, with the result that the natural growth rate of the rural population rose rapidly, reaching 29.47 per thousand in 1965.

Through the implementation of the family planning policy by the government over the past thirty years and more, the natural growth rate of China's population has decreased steadily. Finally, a situation characterized by a low childbearing level was brought about at the end of the 1990s, enabling China's population to transit to the stages of low birth rate, low death rate, and low natural growth rate. This has been called a "later population change." At present, the situation of China's population growth can be expressed briefly as that of: Low fertility rate, high increment.

The natural growth rate of China's population declined from 33 per thousand in 1963 to about 8 per thousand in 2000, representing a pioneering step in human history. This accords with the "Decision of the CPC Central Committee and the State Council On Strengthening Demographic and Family Planning Work, and Stabilizing the Low Birth Level," which stated that over the past fifty years since the founding of the People's Republic of China, particularly since the start of reform and opening up, China's demographic and family planning work has scored remarkable achievements. Under the circumstances of an underdeveloped economy, China has effectively controlled the fast growth of the population, bringing the birth level to below the alternating level and realizing a historic change from a high birth, low death, and high growth rate to a low birth, low death, and low growth rate. The policy has successively blazed a new road with Chinese characteristics for comprehensively tackling the population problem and has thus made an active contribution to stabilizing the growth of the world's population. Thus over the past twenty-odd years, China has given fewer births to a total of around 300 million people, calculated in accordance with the birth level of 1973.

The decline in the death rate has resulted from a rise in the life expectancy of China's population. In old China, the death rate among the population was quite high, standing at about 25-33 per thousand, infant death rates even stood above 200-250 per thousand, and the average life span of the population was only 35 years. Presently, the average life expectancy of China's population has exceeded 70 years, with the male's life expectancy standing at about 70 years and female's at about 74 years, higher than all other developing countries by 10 years. It should be noted that the average life expectancy for females at 74 years is nine years higher than the goal of 65 years by the year 2000 that has been set by the United Nations for the average life expectancy of the world's women. It was said in the past that it was rare for human beings to live up to 70 years. But today, most of the Chinese can live up to over 70 years, as long as no accident happens to them.

3. The Peasantry: Rapidly Changing into the Working Class

Over the past half century and more, since the founding of the People's Republic of China in 1949, urbanization has been the most important event affecting Chinese society.

From the first to the fourth census, the size of China's rural population had undergone a net increase. After the fourth census, the absolute size of the rural population began to decrease. This indicates that there has been acceleration in the flow of rural persons to the cities, as well as the increase in the capability of Chinese cities to absorb the rural population. If population urbanization is seen as an important index of modernization, then China's modernization level has witnessed a marked rise. Some large cities and the overwhelming majority of medium and small cities and towns of China have, since 2000, begun to carry out a reform of the household register system. By the end of 2001, the big cities of China had, to different degrees, carried out a reform of the original household register system, easing policy restrictions on rural residents becoming members of urban households. The curtain had also been raised for the reform of the household register system even in the large cities of Beijing and Shanghai. This reform of the household register system, to a great extent, presages the fact that the speed of China's future urbanization of its population will only accelerate.

Changes in the composition of the urban and rural population have immeasurably led to changes in the relationship of China's class structure. During the period of the traditional planned economy, China's class structure was manifested mainly as two classes plus one stratum (i.e., the working class and the peasantry and the stratum of intellectuals). But the institutional innovation brought about by the drive of reform and opening up has greatly liberated various social strata — especially the peasantry. Along with the success in rural reform and increase in farmers' incomes, the degree of industrialization of the peasantry, with family as the main unit, has witnessed a great change. The rise of township enterprises in rural areas and the shift of agricultural labor to the non-agricultural field have greatly increased the force motivating the peasantry's self-transformation into a working class. The circulation of the labor force among industries, among regions, and between cities and the countryside has, to a certain degree, brought about a change in the vocational category and social status of the peasantry.

This can be clearly seen from the sizes of China's urban and rural population. The proportion of the rural population to China's total population had decreased from 79.4 percent in 1982, during the early period of reform, to 73.77 percent in 1990, and then further to 63.91 percent in 2000. At present, China's rural employees, or workers in the township enterprises, comprise more than 100 million. If the 80 to 100 million farmers who have left the agricultural production field and are now engaged in long-term work in towns and big cities are regarded as part of the working class, then the number of the Chinese farmers is greatly reduced. Estimates show that the proportion of Chinese farmers currently engaged in crop cultivation compared to the total number of employees in the entire society has dropped to about 44 percent. It can thus be surmised that the reform of the household register system now under way will speed this process of the change of China's peasantry into a working class. The size of the Chinese working class has indeed undergone unprecedented growth. This marks the most striking characteristic of the transformation of Chinese classes since the launching of the reform and opening up program.

4. Ethnic Minority Population: Now Exceeding 100 Million

In the early period after the founding of the People's Republic of China, thanks to the implementation of the land reform policy in regions inhabited by the Han people, especially in vast rural areas, the living standards and health conditions of the Han population improved relatively rapidly. This gave a boost to the natural population growth rate. The situation in the ethnic minority areas, however, was rather complicated at that time. The development there was fairly slow in terms of the building up of political power and in the transformation of culture and local customs. Furthermore, the educational level of the ethnic minority areas was relatively low. The number of people receiving a modern education was relatively few, and the pace of improvement in health was fairly slow. As a result, although there was also rapid growth in the populations of various ethnic minority groups during this period, the growth rate was manifestly lower than it was for the Han population.

In the first census of 1953, the proportion of the ethnic minority population to the total population was 6.08 percent. In the second census of 1964, the proportion had dropped to 5.78 percent. At the start of the 1970s, the Chinese government began to implement a strict family planning policy. Only then did the population growth, especially that of the Han population, slow down. In the third census, the proportion of ethnic minority peoples to the total population saw an increase compared to the figure from the second census. The period from the third census in 1982 to the completion of the fourth census in 1990 was a time when the country implemented a strict family planning policy among the Han people, doing its best to control the growth of the population aggregate in inland areas. At the same time, the government relaxed the policy of controlling the growth of the ethnic minority population, especially among certain ethnic minority groups with relatively few people. The government's policy among the minority people allowed one couple to give birth to "two children" or "three children" there. Children of the Hans who had one ethnic minority parent on either the paternal or maternal line were designated as ethnic minority children during this period.

Therefore, in the eight years between the third census and fourth census, the proportion of ethnic minority people to the total population grew the fastest. In 1990, the size of the ethnic minority population in comparison to the total population was 8.04 percent. During the decade from the fourth census in 1990 to the fifth census in 2000, the ethnic minority areas also began to control their excessively rapid population growth, and the growth rate of their population to the total population slowed down. In 2000, the proportion of ethnic minority population to the total population was 8.41 percent, an increase of only 0.37 percentage points compared with the earlier 8.04 percent. The aggregate of the ethnic minority population had reached 106.43 million.

5. The General Cultural Quality: Not Good Enough

Generally speaking, for the population of any country (especially its laboring population), the greater the proportion of people with a high education level, the higher the content of human capital. Thus education contributes greatly to the labor productivity of the population of this country, and is a driving force for economic growth and greater social development.

During the 18 years from the second census to the third, the proportion of the population with a two-year college or higher level of education increased only from 416 to 615 among every 100,000 people. At the same time the number of people with senior high and technical secondary school education showed a rapid growth, increasing from 1,319 to 6,779 among every 100,000 people. But during the eight years from the third census in 1982 to the fourth census in 1990, along with the fast development of China's higher education system, the population with a two-year college or higher level increased rapidly from 615 to 1,422 among every 100,000 persons. During the ten years from the fourth census in 1990 to the fifth census in 2000, the population with a two-year college or higher level of education grew even faster. There was a net increase of 2,189 people calculated on the basis of 3,611 people among a population of every 100,000. It can now be said that education has contributed an inestimable share during China's economic development and social progress since the launch of the reform and opening up project.

An illiterate population or a population with little education not only affects the level of labor productivity, but also seriously retards the progress of a country's modernization. So, in a general sense, the rate of illiteracy presents a negative relationship to economic development and social progress.

During the second census in 1964, the illiteracy rate of China's population was 34 percent. It dropped to 23 percent during the third census and further to 16 percent by the fourth census. Then the figure fell to about 7 percent at the time of the fifth census in 2000. Reducing the illiteracy rate to around 7 percent was a major happening in the history of China. Furthermore, thanks to the implementation of the nine-year compulsory education system, the attendance rate of China's new-born population reached over 99 percent, and China's illiteracy rate had been decreasing among the population aged 15 and over.

Although the population with an educational level of two-year college and above was 3,611 for every 100,000 people in 2000, the distribution of those with a higher education level was extremely uneven. For example, in terms of the difference between the urban and rural areas, the population with an education level of college and above was 8,899 out of every 100,000 people in China's cities and towns, while it was only 492 in the rural areas. There were 21,265 people with a senior high and technical secondary school education level among every 100,000 people in cities and towns, while there were only 5,316 such people in the countryside. In terms of regional differences, the proportion of people with an educational level of two-year college and above compared to the number of people aged at or above 6 years was 17.55 percent in Beijing in 2000, while in the province of Hebei, which is nearby, the proportion was only 2.85 percent. It was 2.59 percent in Guangxi and 2.14 percent in Guizhou.

Although the illiteracy rate of China's total population had dropped to around 7 percent in the year 2000, there existed a striking disparity in the illiteracy rates in different regions. The illiteracy rate was relatively low in north China and the northeast region, with a figure below 5 percent in the overwhelming majority of those provinces. But the illiteracy rate was relatively high in southwest and northwest regions. The illiteracy rates in provinces such as Qinghai, Gansu, Ningxia, Guizhou, and Yunnan were all above 10 percent. Specifically, they were 18.03 percent, 14.34 percent, 13.4 percent, 13.89 percent, and 11.39 percent respectively. Given this situation, the main task in the large-scale development of the western region should be one of raising the educational level of the population and improving the quality of life of the local laboring people. Practice in economic development shows that only a laboring population with a good education can meet the needs of the market and economic competition.

6. Future Pressures on Providing for the Aged

In general terms, when the greater proportion of a country's population is aged between 0 and 14 years, the population of that country is said to be young. When the population aged 0 to 14 gradually decreases and that portion aged between 15 and 64 gradually increases, while the population aged at and above 65 years old stands below 7 percent, then the population is said to be of an "adult type." When the proportion of a country's old people, aged at 65 years or more, exceeds 7 percent in comparison to the total population, then the country is said to have entered the "aging" period. The census conducted in 2000 revealed that the proportion of China's population aged 65 years and older had reached 6.96 percent. This means China is entering the period of an aging society.

During the high-speed growth in the birth rate of China's population between the 1950s and 1960s, the proportion of people aged at 0-14 in comparison to the total population was on the increase, rising from 36.28 percent during the first census period to 40.69 percent during the second census period. After China implemented the family planning policy in the 1970s, along with the decline in the total fertility rate of women, the proportion of people aged between 0-14 steeply fell, diving to 33.59 percent during the third census, 27.69 percent during the fourth census, and 22.89 percent during the fifth census. Aging is a concept of population structure. Aging in China resulted, on the one hand, from the extension of the average life span and, on the other, from the relative reduction in the infant population.

Most people believe that the aging problem is more serious in the cities than in the rural areas, but this is wrong! It is a common mistake based on previous predictions of the condition of aging population, whether made by government departments or demographic circles. These predictions neglected the changes in the urban and rural structures resulting from the migration of population. An examination of previous forecasts shows that the aging of the urban population was more serious than it was in the rural areas. This has been true in some old cities, such as Shanghai. But in the new-type cities, such as Shenzhen, the proportion of the population aged 65 and older to the total population was only a little over 1 percent by the end of 2000. Taking the country as a whole, the actual situation is that the aging level of the urban population is lower than it is in rural areas. It can be said that it was the flow of population, or to be more exact, the flow of young people from the countryside to cities, that effectively alleviated the aging problem in the cities. Added to this, the formidable base number of China's population, despite the "acceleration" of aging, shows that China still can "bear the burden" in the coming twenty years.

Because the proportion of Chinese aged at and above 65 years compared to the total population will be 7.83 percent in 2005, 8.47 percent in 2010, 9.7 percent in 2015 and 11.8 percent in 2020, this will put great pressure on China, but in the near term, it will not be quite as high a pressure.

But in the twenty years between 2020 and 2040, the proportion of people age 65 and older will rapidly increase to around 19 percent. By then, China will face an unprecedented challenge.

7. Employment, Employment, and Still Employment

The proportion of the laboring population aged 15 to 64 compared to the total population has risen rapidly. The 2000 census shows that the proportion of China's population in that age bracket to the total population reached 70.15 percent. By the end of 2001, China had a total of 730 million employees in urban and rural areas, 300 million more than the combined total of 430 million employees in the developed Western countries. Diverse predictions indicate that the proportion of China's future laboring population will remain at a high level of about 70 percent for a long time.

At the same time, an increase in the laboring population implies a growth in the demand for jobs. If the number of jobs provided by society cannot meet the needs of the growth of the laboring population, then China will be plagued by unemployment in the early part of the 21st century. According to demographers, the problem of unemployment cannot be solved within a short space of time. Still less can one expect that the employment pressure to ease in the near future. The government should treat the solving of the unemployment problem as a long-term national policy. The growth of the population aged between 15 and 59 will persist until after 2020 before the rise can probably be halted. The population in this age bracket will reach 920 million in the year 2010, and there will be a net increase of 100 million in the laboring population in comparison to what it is at present. By the year 2020, it will further increase to 940 million. That is to say, in the next twenty-odd years. China will need to create job opportunities for the newly added 120 million people to overcome the problem concerning existing unemployed people and to solve the employment problem of the laid-off workers.

Since in the 1990s, the employment question has stood out as one of the most important issues facing Chinese society.

The registered urban unemployed population was 3.939

million and the registered unemployment rate was 2.3 percent in 1992; 4.201 million and 2.5 percent in 1993; 4.764 million and 2.8 percent in 1994; 5.196 million and 2.9 percent in 1995; 5.528 million and 3 percent in 1996; 5.5758 million and 3.1 percent in 1997; and 5.95 million and 3.1 percent in 2000. By the end of 2001, the registered urban unemployment rate went up to 3.6 percent; and further to 3.7 percent in March 2002. If the registered unemployed population includes the laid-off workers, then the unemployment rate increased to about 7 percent in 2000, and the figure was even higher in 2001. From recent statistics it can be seen that the re-employment rate for laid-off workers has begun to slide downwards. The figures for the urban unemployment rate do not include the 150 million surplus rural laborers.

In the past, China suffered a great deal from unemployment; educated youth went to work in the mountain areas and the countryside, and laid-off workers from state-owned enterprises brought a great deal of pressure on the country. At present, China is experiencing an adjustment of the economic structure. The question of unemployment and employment has become a great, overriding matter.

The most important achievement gained since the introduction of the reform and opening up program in China is the successful solving of the problem of feeding and clothing the nearly 1.3 billion population. At present, China is, through its steady development, solving the employment problem for the laboring population that represents 26 percent of the world's total laboring population. The whole world is focusing its attention on this issue.

To solve the problem of unemployment, the following two points should be taken into consideration: first, particular attention should be paid to developing labor-intensive enterprises with a market potential. Second, ways should be pursued to achieve full employment. Under certain circumstances, there do exist contradictions between efficiency and full employment, but is it possible to find a balanced point of social development between efficiency and full employment? This is a subject worth studying.

8. An Old Topic of Conversation

When talking about the impact of China's entry into the WTO, a well-known scholar has said: This is neither the Purple Air coming from the east (a propitious omen) nor fierce floods and savage beasts (great scourges), but rather it is an integration of opportunities and challenges. This remark appears to be more appropriate when the influence of the WTO on employment and unemployment is taken into consideration. A major subject of recent academic discussions is whether WTO accession will increase employment or increase unemployment. Of course the initial issue in such talks originates from two foreign predictions:

The first is an optimistic prediction, holding that the WTO entry could immediately create efficiency. According to the estimate by the UN Conference on Trade and Development (UNCTAD), China's entry into the WTO could increase the GDP by 2.94 percentage points. And each percentage-point increase in the GDP could create an additional 4 million job opportunities, i.e., a 3 percentage-point increase would bring about 12 million more jobs.

The second prediction, though rather pessimistic, is full of development prospects. According to the evaluation of the Washington International Economic Research Institute, China's WTO accession, with the accompanying tariff reduction and a full opening to the import of agricultural and industrial products, would lead to the unemployment of 11 million people. But several years later, the labor and capital market would once again be full of vigor, thereby increasing jobs.

China's domestic academic circles take an attitude of compatibility toward these two kinds of predications. The basis for the simultaneous tenability of these two opposite judgments lies in this matter: the circulation of elements after the opening of the factor market, compared with the competitiveness of the Chinese labor market, which one is in a superior position. That is to say, if economic expansion can further increase the ability to absorb manpower, then it can create more job opportunities; but if the economy is not expanded and its ability to take in the labor force remains unchanged or is in a disadvantageous position in terms of competition, then an increase in imports could likewise lead to an increase in unemployment.

For the automobile, machinery, cereals and edible oil processing, electronic communication equipment, electrical machinery, instrument and meter, metallurgy, petroleum and natural gas, and coal mining industries, these would possibly face a grim situation in terms of competition by drawing back from development, thus leading to the "dismissal" of the original workers and staff members of these industries and a reduction of millions of jobs. But for the textile, commerce, construction, chemical, food processing, and leather manufacturing industries, as well as for the service industries, these would possibly expand in a short space of time and absorb more employees, increasing millions and even tens of millions of jobs. Generally speaking, China will face many challenges in the near term, but some more jobs will be created in the long term. The prerequisite for this is the smooth development of labor-intensive enterprises.

The WTO will exert a greater impact in rural areas and on agriculture and farming laborers. China's crop cultivation, in particular, previously lacked international competitiveness because of its high price and poor quality. But at present, great changes have taken place in the agricultural structure. In mega-agriculture (farming, forestry, animal husbandry, and fisheries), the output value of crops accounted for only a little more than one half of the products produced, and for crops, the proportions of fruit, vegetable, oil crops, flower and grass, tobacco, tea, and other products became bigger and bigger. These factors should create job opportunities as a result of the expansion of exports. So, as long as China speeds up the pace of adjustment in the structure of the agricultural sector, it will be possible to reduce the negative impact on agriculture.

The WTO entry will accelerate China's globalization process. In order to maintain the recently gained favorable position in the course of global competition and effectively solve the unemployment problem, the following two points must be taken into consideration:

First, China must universally extend the length of education for laborers, increase the deposit of the country's human capital and adapt it to scientific and technological progress, mitigate the current employment pressures, and reduce the range of capital's exclusion of the labor force.

Second, China must continue to retain the competitiveness of the laborers' wages and maintain the trend of shifting the world's manufacturing center to China.

9. The Blood-tied Family: Changing into a Marriage-tied Family

In this nearly 3,000-year-old agricultural society, the structure and scale of Chinese families have never before experienced major changes. Yet, since 1949 and the establishment of the socialist system, there has begun a reform in many internal functional structures of the family, thus enabling women to genuinely walk out of their doors and gain unprecedented emancipation in society. This has constituted a great threat to the patriarchal and manus systems.

But the change in the family structure has still been slow. Politically, the superstructure compulsory reform of the family system was much inferior to the economic base's rapid change in its established structure. Since the start of reform and opening up, the market economy has also opened a new era for the family revolution and has thereby accelerated the change from blood-tied relations as being the primary factor in Chinese families to the marriage-tied relationship as the primary factor. The most remarkable feature brought about by this change has been a diminution in the size of each family.

The birth rate among the population resulted in a rapid rise in the size of each household during the 1950s. But due to the rise in the death rates during the three difficult years caused by the Great Leap Forward, the per-household scale of Chinese families was reduced. The birth rates after 1962 and 1963 once again began to push up the size of the families. This trend of growth continued till the mid-1970s and then it rapidly declined only under the influence of the family planning policy. The per-household population during the fourth census in 1990 was 3.96 persons and it was 3.44 persons during the fifth census in 2000.

In the process of establishing marriage-tied families, Chinese family life is increasingly demonstrating the following ten major tendencies:

First, the enormous control on family fertility has led to a steep reduction in the number of children born to couples. This was manifested in one couple one child in cities and towns, and about two children per couple in the rural areas.

Second, the large families of youth and adults are changing into nuclear families, while households containing aged persons are being emptied: whether in villages or in cities, grown-up children, after marriage, prefer to live separately as much as possible. Even for the children, their time of living in families is getting shorter due to study or work. Many couples, at the age of forty or more, see their children leaving their families for other places in order to seek their own development.

Third, traditional blood-tied families are changing into modern marriage-tied families. The proportion of the parent-offspring relationship is being reduced, whereas the husband-wife relationship is becoming the only lasting tie in the family relationships.

Fourth, the age for a first marriage is being postponed again and again, while there is an increase in the number of persons who do not plan to be married, and the speed of young rural women moving to the cities is increasing.

Fifth, the responsibility of providing for the aged is being shifted from their children to the spouses supporting themselves. Among older couples, the younger and healthier ones are undertaking the main service of caring for and spiritually consoling the older ones. They rely upon each other in daily life from the beginning of the "empty nest" to an age of over seventy years. With the decrease in the number of children, the industry of looking after the aged is developing rapidly, and the mode of "hiring hands to take care of the aged" has emerged.

Sixth, the concept of marriage is changing, husbands and wives are no longer viewing themselves as just "make-do partners," and the divorce rate will remain high for a long period of time.

Seventh, the status of females in the family is rising, and husbands and wives are becoming more and more equal in status.

Eighth, the proportion of the education investment in family expenditures is becoming ever larger.

Ninth, the family economy or clan economy still has vitality, and the reproduction function of the family economy will persist.

Tenth, the proportion of single-person families, single-parent families, remarried families, and families with only a husband and a wife will increase.

10. Future Chinese Population: to Be Less Than 1.55 Billion

How large will China's future total population be? This is one of the issues of most concern in today's world.

During the entire 1990s, a basic understanding was formed around China's future total population, both in academic circles and in the mass media, that it would peak at around 1.6 billion and should reach this apex around the year 2050.

Discussion of the question regarding food security was almost inseparable from this specious conclusion. Even in the discussion on China's sustainable development, scholars and government officials looked upon the figure of 1.6 billion as the "final conclusion." Predictability is, after all, "prediction," and who can give an exact answer to the question regarding population size fifty years from now? Even in near term population forecasts, demographic circles are unable to give a relatively "credible" presumption.

For example, the overwhelming majority of predictions have likely overestimated China's population aggregate in 2000. Many predictions made either by the United Nations or by domestic research institutes put the total population on the Chinese mainland at between 1.27 and 1.28 billion. The result of the fifth census, however, revealed that the figure was 1.265 billion, a difference as great as over 10 million. As it now turns out, scholars have underestimated the degree of the decline in the total birth rate resulting from the practice of family planning, have underestimated the restrictive factors of population growth brought about by urbanization, and underestimated the rate of China's urbanization.

Although major estimates of the base number of the total population in 2000 were made in the various predictions, it was discovered that the peaked value of China's future population would not reach 1.6 billion. If the actual population of the Chinese mainland was considered to be 1.265 billion in 2000, and it was believed that no major adjustment would be made to the current family planning policy in the near term, then China's future population aggregate would not reach 1.6 billion, but rather would possibly stand at around 1.55 billion. The peaked value should come about at around the year 2040. In the near term, China's population aggregate in 2010 would not reach the planned controlled target of 1.4 billion, but possibly would stand at around 1.37-1.38 billion.

If China's future urbanization develops faster, and young people's marriage age is further postponed, then the birthrate of population will somewhat decline. In that case, China's aging speed will be faster than predicted. Under such circumstances, the task of population control should be focused on structural readjustment and quality-oriented education.

(Written by Zhang Yi)

Chapter 3 Education

In 1992, the 14th National Congress of the Chinese Communist Party put forth the principle that "The development of education is the fundamental policy for the realization of China's modernization." In 1997, the 15th National Congress of the CPC stated that it was important to adopt "the strategy of developing China by relying on science and education and the strategy of sustainable development as one for economic and social development in the 21st century to build socialism with Chinese characteristics." For the first time, education as the fundamental policy superseded economic development, which was unheard until then. Even so, China's education still has a long way to go.

By 2000, China with a population of 1.27 billion, making it the most populous country in the world, had found itself with an average schooling per capita at only about eight years. China obviously lagged behind developed countries. China's population is now expected to reach 1.5 billion by the year of 2021, so the country faces an arduous task to bridge the gap. During the next twenty years, about 400 million youth will enter the labor market. The prosperity and development of the country and the future of the nation directly hinges on the quality of its educational system.

1. Education: Enjoying Financial Increments by a Large Margin

"It takes ten years to grow trees but a hundred years to foster capable people," as the Chinese saying goes. It is hard to evaluate comprehensively the effect of education reform. Nevertheless, the past ten years did witness the fastest development in education since the founding of the People's Republic of China in 1949, as the whole country and nation have attached great importance to education.

In 1992, the 14th National Congress of the Chinese Communist Party put forth the principle that "The development of education is the fundamental policy for the realization of China's modernization." And in 1997, the 15th National Party Congress stated that "The development of education and science is the basis for culture." Training hundreds of millions of workers of high caliber and tens of millions of capable people with expertise so as to bring into play the huge potential of China's human resources is a goal closely related to the socialist cause in the 21st century. It is imperative to place education in the position of being a strategic priority for development. The strategy is one of developing China by relying on science and education and the strategy of sustained development is one for economic and social development in the 21st century so as to build socialism with Chinese characteristics. For the first time in history, education as the fundamental policy has superseded economic development.

"Leaders who neglect education are immature leaders without a vision and cannot lead the modernization drive. Leaders at various levels should do a good job in educational work as well as in economic work." "We should try by every means possible to solve educational problems, even if we have to give up something in other fields at the expense of the speed of development." These incisive and clarion sayings were by Mr. Deng Xiaoping, who laid down the theoretical foundation for the priority development and financial support of education.

In the past twenty years since the introduction of the reform and opening up program in 1978, governments at various levels made great efforts to increase financial support under the conditions of a tight budget. From 1978 to 1998, the state financial expenditure increased by 850 percent, from 112.2 billion yuan to 1,071.1 billion yuan, while the education expenditures under the budget increased by 19.6 times from 7.62 billion yuan to 156.55 billion yuan. Education expenditures in 1978 accounted for 6.8 percent of the total financial expenditures and increased to 14.53 percent.

The biggest increase in education financing came about during the past few years. The central authorities decided to increase the education expenditures in the total financial budget by 1 percent each year for five consecutive years from 1998. Most provinces and municipalities followed suit. The national expenditure in education climbed from the low point of 2.41 percent of the national GDP in 1995 to 3.19 percent in 2001. This reduced the gap in comparison with that of 4.1 percent in developing countries, according to the statistics of UNESCO in 1998. The total national input for education in 2001 was 384.908 billion yuan, an increase of 105 percent over the 187.795 billion in 1995. The budgetary appropriation for education in 2001 was 208.568 billion yuan, an increase of 75 percent over the 119.38 billion in 1995.

The financial increment put into education improved the conditions in running the schools. The floor space for primary and high schools saw a rapid increase, while the number of school buildings in need of major repairs went down sharply from 13 percent of the total floor space in 1980 to 1 percent in 1998. The budget for every student increased, while the equipment for education, research, and library books was refurbished and updated.

Yet the situation of insufficient finance in education and lack of education resources has not fundamentally changed. Though the education expenditure for 2001 accounted for 3.19 percent, as against the 2.14 percent in 1995, and additional measures to raise education funds by non-government input accounted for 38.4 percent in 2000 from 25.7 percent in 1990, yet the percentage for public education lagged far behind that of the world average. At the end of the 20th century, the world average was 4.8 percent, 5 to 6 percent for developed countries and more than 4 percent for developing countries.

2. The Heavy Task of Consolidating and Upgrading "the Two Basics"

The basic principles of popularizing the 9-year compulsory education program and elimination of illiteracy throughout the whole country (abbreviated as "the two basics") were goals set forth by the State Council for education reform and development in the 1990s. This was the most important priority in education for upgrading the national quality.

Under the guidance of the policy of "taking initiative, seeking truth from facts, planning according to regional location, offering specific guidance, and implementing this step by step," great headway has been made with concerted efforts from all fields. By the end of 2001, 2,571 counties had attained the goal of "the two basics". All the counties (including municipalities and districts) of the 11 cities and provinces of Beijing, Tianjin, Shanghai, Jiangsu, Guangdong, Zhejiang, Liaoning, Jilin, Fujian, Shandong and Hebei had achieved "the two basics." A total of 85 percent of the national population was covered by "the two basics," with 88.6 percent of those eligible entering junior middle school. The number of illiterates among the young and middle-aged had been lowered to under 30 million from 61.71 million in 1990. Adult illiteracy was down 130 million from 182 million in 1990. And 85.5 percent of the adult population was able to read, up from 77.7 percent. The task of "the two basics" was thus being fulfilled.

The realization of "the two basics" was a complicated, arduous, and glorious cause for China, a big country with a population of 1.3 billion and a relatively weak foundation in education and economy. This achievement was recognized by countries over the world and highly praised by international institutions such as the World Bank and UNESCO.

China has made historical progress and in the meantime faces some serious problems. By the year of 2000, 520 counties out of a national total of more than 2,000 had not yet attained the goal of 9-year compulsory education, and among these, 100 counties had not achieved the goal of 6-year compulsory education. There were 85 million illiterate adults in China, more than 20 million of whom were young and middle-aged. They were concentrated in poor and remote areas and places where ethnic minorities live. This posed an even harder job. In the meantime, the rate of dropouts from junior middle schools in rural areas remained high and the imminent peak age group eligible for junior middle school education intensified the contradictions between supply and demand in the field of education.

Compulsory education in rural areas has long been the responsibility of the counties and towns and farmers themselves. Quite a few poor localities with limited financial resources found it hard to shoulder the responsibility of developing a program of local compulsory education. The shortage of expenditures for compulsory education and rural schools began to worsen and much of the floor space in the primary and middle school buildings in danger were on the increase. Conditions in some schools of 9-year compulsory education deteriorated. Courses and programs for eliminating illiteracy could not meet the needs of farmers, nor could they bring into play their enthusiasm for education. In June of 2000, the State Council issued a "decision on the reform and development of elementary education." It set forth the new goal that counties take the major responsibility in the management of rural compulsory education so as to strengthen management at the county governmental levels. In the meantime, the central and provincial governments transferred more payments to the localities with financial difficulties. This somewhat alleviated the problem. Nevertheless, the task of "the two basics" will remain the paramount priority in education for a quite long period, and so will unremitting efforts toward this goal.

3. From Examination-oriented Education to Quality Education

Since the mid-1990s, people have begun to embrace the concept of quality education as a fundamental aim. But due to a number of reasons, there has been a tendency of using education as just a matter of "learning for examinations." This impedes the implementation of quality education and training to produce people of high caliber and creativity.

The "Outline for Education Development and Reform," issued in 1993 by the State Council, pointed out that primary and middle schools should turn "examination-oriented education onto the track of education to upgrade the quality of the people." The "Decision on Deepening Education Reform and Thoroughly Pushing Forward Education for Quality," issued in 1999, elaborated this program of education for quality and set forth a series of important measures.

Education for quality is a profound reform in the traditional ideology of education and obsolete education concepts. It cannot be achieved overnight, though great efforts have been made in this respect during recent years.

First, there has been acceleration in the reform of teaching materials and in upgrading teaching content. A new system of elementary courses was put on trial in the fall of 2001. An "Outline of the Reform of Elementary Teaching Courses (Trial Edition)" was issued and standard courses of compulsory education (experiment) were distributed. Also research and experiment on new courses for senior high schools took on full steam. In the fall of 2001, 26 municipalities and provinces began the trial use of the first group of new textbooks. Redundant and outdated content had been deleted, while the most recent knowledge in the development of science and technology was added. The situation of textbooks being separated from practice and daily life was improved. Primary schools began to teach foreign languages and information technology courses. Green certificate education was pushed in the rural areas. All these improvements have become important parts of the new textbooks.

Second, there has been a reform in the appraisal system of examinations for college enrollment. The reform of college entrance examinations includes changes in the subjects for examination, pushing the program of "3+X," and ways of paper reading. The key has been in computer reading of the papers and enrollment through the Internet. This has made the college entrance examinations more reasonable, fair, and just. The reform of the content of the examinations has placed the emphasis on checking the capability and quality of the examinees. As for the ways of examining, there is a trial reform in holding the examinations twice a year. The reform in college entrance examinations is well under way and is gradually becoming popular and acceptable. It is necessary to probe further to develop scientific methods of appraisal so as to reduce the burden on primary and middle school students and ensure their healthy mental and physical development.

Third, there has been an improvement in teaching methods and modes. It is important to train students in developing creative spirits and practical skills, to encourage students to participate and to be eager to study, and to develop their research skills.

Fourth, there has been an upgrading of modern teaching techniques and information in education.

Fifth, there has been an increase in the number of teachers.

What is more important is the need to attach importance to the adjustment of macro-structure in education, to adopt different approaches to develop high school and higher learning institutions, and to increase enrollment so as to alleviate the tension of competition. It is necessary to build highway bridges favorable for the nurturing of talented people and to create an external environment conducive to quality education.

Education for quality is making headway, step by step, though there are still misunderstandings and difficulties.

4. Common Folk Benefiting from Enlarged College Enrollment

Four years ago, many families welcomed the glad tidings when word came that the universities were ready to enlarge their enrollments. In 1998, the rate for primary school enrollment was 99.3 percent, the gross enrollment rate for junior middle school students was 87.3 percent, that for senior high school students was 41 percent, and that for university students was 9.8 percent. Along with the gradual reaching of the strategic goal of "the two basics," the rate of enrollment for primary and middle schools was quite satisfactory, while that for senior high school and university was still quite low. The State Council made strategic and timely decisions to further enlarge the enrollments in the institutions of higher learning so as to meet the increasing demand.

In 1998, the colleges and universities of the whole nation enrolled 2.157 million students. There were 2.842 million newly enrolled students for 1999 and 3.9 million students for 2000. In 2001, 4.64 million students entered colleges and universities, including 2.68 million for regular colleges and universities and 1.96 million for adult colleges, which was an increase of 925,900 and 913,800 respectively over the enrollment figures for 1995, or an increase of 183 percent and 114 percent. The college enrollment rate for those between 18 to 22 years of age increased to 13.3 percent in 2001 from 7.2 percent in 1995. The enlarged enrollment over the years became one of the most influential events for the social and economic development as well as for the daily lives of the Chinese people.

The enlarged enrollments met the demands for education by students and parents. Three consecutive years of enlarged enrollment had 1.6 million students on the campus, an increase of over 100 percent with an annual increase of 34 percent. In the 13 years from 1985 to 1998, a total increase of 460,000 students with an averaged annual increase of 4.4 percent.

Moreover, the enlarged enrollment promoted reforms in higher education. It changed from purely meeting the demand for educated personnel by the state to meeting the needs of the masses. It urged institutions of higher learning to be within the reach of society, which helped the optimization of colleges and universities. It promoted reforms in the education system, particularly those related to the development of privately-run educational institutions. For instance, in 1998, there were only 16 schools run by the society that were eligible to issue certificates, and by the end of 2001 there were 89 institutions eligible to do so.

Through the investment in people and attaching importance to education, the enlarged enrollment met the increasing demands for higher education, and pushed forward the popularization of higher education. It sped up the development in higher education by 10 to 15 years.

5. A Big Country, Not a Big Power in Higher Education

The enlarged enrollment in college widened the threshold

for students. However, the enrollment by top-notch universities such as Peking University and Tsinghua University is limited. Each student will choose a school or subject according to his or her examination qualifications, interest, and likes. Along with the transformation process toward a socialist market economy, China is intensifying the construction of first-rate universities and institutions of higher learning, endeavoring to rationalize the division of labor among institutions of higher learning, and providing opportunities for diversified choice for common people to go to colleges.

Colleges and universities, in fact, are often divided into academic and professional institutions, whose function and service target are quite different and so are their management and development. Internationally there are three types of colleges. First, universities with high academic expertise and research capabilities that place emphasis on both teaching and research, as well as undergraduate and graduate studies. Second, universities with teaching as the main task that mainly provide undergraduate studies. Third, specialized schools, community colleges, and vocational colleges that mainly train students in skills and practical knowledge. These three types of colleges and universities, with different financial input and conditions, have different research capabilities and academic levels and put different emphases on their students. They play different roles and shoulder different tasks in the whole educational system.

The old mode of an elite education in institutions of higher learning made it impossible for many universities and colleges to meet the diversified needs of society. On the one hand big cities were too crowded for the graduates to find jobs, while on the other, small cities and towns that were desperately in need of college graduates but could not get any. Facing the challenges posed by the market and human resources, institutions of higher learning have continued their efforts in reform so as to break away from the single mode of running schools through categorizing schools and adjusting courses to satisfy the diversified needs of society with diversified educational forms.

Through the building of first-rate universities with key science majors as an academic vanguard that may intensify innovation in science and technology and new knowledge education, a core group will be brought up to advance China's science and technology to a world level. China is a big country but not a great power in education and higher learning. To encourage the establishment of first-rate universities, the Central Government, on the basis of the "211 Project," decided as of 1998 to earmark 1 percent out of the education expenditures of Central Government finance each year as a special fund to support certain universities so that they can become advanced universities on a world level. Now over thirty universities have received this financial support. This not only benefits the expansion of university education to meet the needs of expertise of a high caliber in economic development and the creation of new type job opportunities, but also helps China enhance its comprehensive power and international competitiveness.

Active development of community, vocational, and technical colleges lowered the threshold of higher education and trained a large number of practical workers for the production, service, and management positions that were needed by local enterprises, organizations, and rural communities. In order to promote a positive, diversified development of vocational education in the higher learning institutions, the state delegated the authority to establish vocational and technical colleges to the provincial governments. By 2001, there were 386 special vocational and technical colleges with 720,000 students. All the universities and colleges in China accommodate a total of 6.39 million students in 2 to 3 years' programs, accounting for 54.4 percent of the total number of college students throughout the nation.

6. A Decade of Rapid Development of Privately-run Education

The rapid development of privately-run education in the past years has provided more opportunities for people to choose. After the founding of the People's Republic of China, the country carried out a planned economy and a reform policy over private schools (church schools). From 1951 to 1952, middle schools and colleges that had received foreign subsidies had their subsidies revoked. From 1952 to 1954, all the private primary and middle schools were turned into public schools. This developed into the system of government running education that lasted until the opening and reform program initiated in the late 1970s. Private schools in China then went from none to a few and then to many becoming an important component in China's education and an indispensable force for educational reform.

By the end of 2001, there were 56,274 private schools or educational institutions approved by the educational administrations at various levels, with 9.23 million students and 42,000 teachers. There were 44,526 private kindergartens, accounting for 39.9 percent of the total; 4,846 private primary schools or 1 percent of the national total; 4,571 private middle schools or 5.7 percent of the total; and 1,202 private higher learning institutions, 89 of which were qualified to issue diplomas approved or authorized by the Ministry of Education, and 436 institutions that had the right to give examinations for diploma.

The private schools are developing in a diversified manner and cover the educational levels from kindergarten to college. The school managers are appointed in either sole or cooperative management by various groups, including democratic parties, societies, institutions, private citizens, and overseas personages. A multi-layered, flexible, comprehensive system of education is thus taking form.

Private schools are products of a market economy. The quality of education in these schools is directly involved with their survival and development, so the competition is extraordinarily tense.

It is well known that several of the retired teachers started their schools by leasing private houses in which to establish them in the 1980s. Now the new generation has the advantage of their higher educational background, courage, and new concepts. These people, with vision, are not content with short-term interests but attach importance to financial investment and high quality. They are the mainstay and hope for the education system by private schools.

Of course the education run by non-government sectors is still at the stage of upgrading quality, intensifying school management, and building up credit with a good reputation. The joint development between private schools and public education has a long way to go, and still needs gigantic efforts to succeed.

On the 24th of June, 2002, the 28th meeting of the Standing Committee of the National People's Congress reviewed the draft of the "Law on the Promotion of Education by the Private Sector of the People's Republic of China." The purpose of this law is to establish the role of privately-run education within the socialist education system, to regulate private school activities and administrative management, to protect the legal rights of the teachers and students as well as of supporters of private schools, and to promote the healthy and sound development of education run by the private sector. The issuance of the law will inevitably give impetus to achieving bigger strides.

7. What Does Annual Salary of One Million for a Teacher Signify?

In the past, the mentality of "refusing to earn a living by teaching so long as there is some grain at home" prevailed. But during the past few years, an unprecedented phenomenon took shape, namely, more and more students began to register as students of normal schools and the basic quality of these students was getting higher. In the meantime, not only normal school graduates but also graduates of comprehensive colleges and universities were willing to choose teaching as their profession. The profession of teaching provided a stable job with good pay and respect, which contributed mainly to the change in attitudes about the profession of teaching.

Advertisements were posted in newspapers and periodicals to recruit teachers with a better pay for the universities, middle and primary schools, and even kindergartens. In order to get overseas students to return to teach, many provincial and municipal governments held employment conferences to invite them with promises of preferential treatment if they would return to teach or do research. Officials in some provinces even led delegations that went abroad to directly employ talented people. On the 28th of April of 2002, Tsinghua University issued certificates of employment to 28 overseas Chinese scholars. It was reported that they would work for 3 to 4 months each year in the Economic Management College with an annual pay of 1 million yuan each. For a period of time, an "annual salary of 1 million yuan for teachers" became a hot topic among the people. The concept of teaching as an admirable profession is now becoming a reality.

Twenty years ago, the basic attitude was that there were insufficient teachers. It was believed that they were an unstable labor force, that they merited little respect, and could be treated poorly. This was particularly true for primary and middle school teachers. Besides this, there was the historically leftover problem of teachers-not-on-the-government-payroll.

According to statistics, the primary, junior, and senior middle school teachers who were qualified to teach according to the "Teachers Law" went from 47.1 percent, 9.8 percent, and 45.9 percent in 1978 to 96.81 percent, 88.72 percent, and 70.71 percent in 2001. In the meantime, young and middle-aged teachers became the backbone of those in primary and middle schools.

Teachers-not-on-the-government-payroll was a special form of employment with Chinese characteristics. In 1978, there were 4.6545 million teachers who were not on the government payroll, accounting for 55.3 percent of the total number of teachers. In the mid-1980s, governments at various levels took measures to solve the problem in line with the policy of "to close, to transfer, to recruit, to dismiss, and to retire". In June of 1994, at a national educational work conference, the Central Government explicitly laid down the goal of basically solving the problem by the end of the 20th century. According to statistics, since the mid-1980s, approximately 2.12 million qualified teachers-not-on-the-government-payroll were transferred to teachers of public schools after they passed examinations; about 710,000 teachers-not-on-the-government-payroll were recruited to the middle normal schools; around 660,000 unqualified teachers were dismissed after they failed the examinations; and over 200,000 teachers retired. So far, the great majority of the provinces have solved the problem of teachers-not-on-the-government-payroll.

The "Teachers Law" issued in October of 1993 clearly stipulated for the first time an examination system for teachers. Various regions, in line with "Rules on the Management of the Qualification Certificates for Teachers," carried out verification of the qualifications of teachers either on the job or about to be hired. This means that teaching as a profession, like that of lawyers, doctors, and accountants, requires a qualification certificate.

In order to have the training of teachers keep in pace with the development of the times, the Ministry of Education has, since 1999, adjusted the structure of normal schools and gradually upgraded the training of teachers and teaching degrees for education. An educational system of teachers with current normal schools as the mainstay and the participation of other colleges and universities is being established and gradually perfected.

In recent years the salaries and benefits for teachers increased by a relatively big margin. In 1999, the average annual wage for members of the faculty was 8,474 yuan, an increase of 56 percent over that of 1995. Local governments guaranteed to give primary and middle school teachers full payment on time and their housing conditions improved greatly. Teaching became a stable and admirable profession in society.

8. Education for the Disadvantaged Group of People

The Central Government has constantly attached importance to financial aid for college students whose families have economic difficulties. As of 1994, a total of 1.045 billion yuan from the reserve funds of the Premier of the State Council and emergency financial appropriations were used to support college students with economic difficulties at colleges and universities under the central ministries. Since 1987, the Ministry of Education, Ministry of Finance, and governments at various levels have been committed to establishing a policy to give financial aid to students whose families have economic difficulties. These include scholarships, student loans, work-study programs, special subsidies, and tuition waivers. The Ministry of Education demands that all colleges and universities establish a "green passage" for freshmen who have economic difficulties. These freshmen will register first and then be given financial aid after verification. In the meantime, local governments at various levels are raising funds through different channels to give financial aid to college students in various forms. The system of student loans has gained support from all fields and is welcomed by the vast number of students.

To guarantee that there are no drop-outs of primary and middle school students in the poor areas, the Chinese government stipulated in 2001 that the poor counties at both the national and provincial levels experiment with "a single sum of fees," namely, on the basis of clearing out exorbitant charges in rural primary and middle schools and strictly verifying the standards of tuition and textbook costs. The central departments concerned, taking into consideration the basic need for general knowledge and English teaching in rural primary and middle schools, set a maximum ceiling for these charges, and made sure that there would be no additional charges. The maximum ceiling on "a single sum of fees" for 2002 is 160 yuan per rural primary school student per year, and 260 yuan per middle school student per year. Provincial governments, with consideration to their economic development, the educational needs, and people's ability to accept, may appropriately adopt a sliding scale of charges of 20 percent and under. This helped reduce the economic burden on rural families with primary and middle school students.

In recent years, China has adopted a more favorable attitude towards the education of the weaker group of people:

— In 1995, the state organized and carried out the first "project of compulsory education in the poverty regions," and the second in 2001. The Central Government put in 8.9 billion yuan for the two projects, for which 6.07 billion yuan was given to the nine provinces and autonomous regions where minority ethnic peoples are concentrated.

— In 1997, the country established a "people's scholarship for compulsory education," and an accumulated 130 million yuan was given to students of minority ethnic families with economic difficulties over four years.

— Textbooks were provided to primary and middle school students whose families were short of income; waived or partially waived tuition fees, boarding charges, and living expenses were provided for these students.

— Tibetan student classes in inland cities were conducted. In 17 years, a total of 24,294 junior middle school students, 15,666 senior middle school or normal school students, and 3,496 college students attended the classes.

— Xinjiang student classes have been conducted in 12 cities such as Beijing and Shanghai since 2000, altogether 2,000 junior middle school graduates of ethnic minority groups from Xinjiang have been recruited for high schools in these 12 cities.

— Aid projects to schools and regions in the western part of China to be carried out. The eastern and western parts each have designated 1,000 schools to participate in the projects, and participating persons and equipment are well prepared. There will be activities like a "program to aid colleges and universities in western China," "education and technology exhibitions in China's west," and "senior visiting scholar programs in colleges and universities in China's west."

— Bilingual teaching activities. About 10,000 schools nationwide use bilingual education courses with a total of 6 million students of all minority ethnic groups.

— Mainly ordinary schools run special classes for handicapped and retarded children, with special schools for these groups of children as the core.

— Compulsory education for the children of migrant populations to be increased. Since the 1990s, along with the industrialization, urbanization, and modernization, large numbers of people are migrating from the countryside to the cities in search of work, nearly 150 million people at present. In the meantime, a large number of migrant children are in need of schooling. It is unthinkable to let the children of the migrant population become new illiterates.

The guarantee of compulsory education for migrant children has become a pressing and important task in the popularization of 9-year compulsory education.

The "Decision on the Reform and Development of Elementary Education by the State Council" issued in May of 2001 said that it is imperative to solve the problem of compulsory education for migrant children. Local governments that take in these migrant people should take the major responsibility for running public primary and middle schools and should adopt various methods to guarantee the rights of the children of the migrant population to an education.

At present, the solution to this problem is mainly done through the following approaches. First, for them to be recruited as guest students in public schools. Second, for them to be enrolled in private schools. Third, for them to go to simple and rudimentary schools. Local governments and educational administrations should give due support and assistance to those schools that have relatively good teaching and conditions so as to help them standardize their teaching activities, and they should abolish those schools that have extremely poor conditions and are far below the teaching standards.

9. IT: Opening up a New Era in Education

The wave of information technology has had a sweeping impact on the whole educational climate and has given impetus to educational modernization. It has become the inevitable road to greater development. Along with video projection on the campuses, information technology has gradually become the new benchmark for the education reform in various countries in the world. The revolution in new technology has triggered important reforms and has had a far-reaching impact on all realms of education.

The development of China's educational information technology in the past ten years has gone through the following three steps as far as the majority of schools are concerned. First, the schools bought a couple of personal computers for office use. Second, they set up computer labs for students to learn how to use computers, and later these became multi-media computer labs for the teaching of various courses. Third, on the basis of the multi-media computer labs, school web sites were set up to be connected with the Internet and to share resources on the net.

The past five years have witnessed the accelerating development of educational information technology. It has progressed from the thriving development of remote education in higher learning institutions with the establishment of several dozens of Internet colleges to the requirement of 15 to 30 percent of the courses being taught via multi-media in colleges; from the popularization of education about information technology in primary and middle schools to the opening up of information technology courses and to implementation of standards for new courses in information technology. All these have shown that China's educational system is catching up with the tide of educational information technology in the developed countries.

China, as a developing country with an effort to bridge the "digital gap," has shown to the world a leap in the development of education. According to statistics about elementary education, in 1999, nearly 60,000 primary and middle schools had computer courses, and by the end of 2001, an additional 10,000 more. There were 3,000 schools with school web sites in 1999, and 11,071 schools with web sites by the end of 2001, with more than 1 million sets of computers in the primary and middle schools. Besides this, 450 colleges and universities were linked to the Internet and the China Education and Science web site. The Internet of the China Education and Science web site reached 160 cities with over 900 educational and research institutions that were equipped with 1.2 million computers and 8 million accounts. This is the second largest Internet network after China Telecom.

10. Toward Life-long Learning

President Jiang Zemin pointed out that the Chinese nation has a fine tradition of respect for education and China in the 21st century should become a country where everybody is keen to learn. What does this mean? The theory of life-long learning is based on modern information and information technology. It is in line with international education standards and economic and social development to meet the educational needs of the all the citizens.

Life-long learning gradually became the order of the day in China as the country entered the 21st century. During the past twenty years of reform and opening up, China's production of materials has become abundant, but the Chinese people have felt a shortage of good quality of education. With the rapid development in science and technology, it has become necessary to study so as to keep abreast of the times. Everybody needs to improve and perfect themselves through learning and the study of the economic transformation from a planned economy to a market economy, the opening and reform and China's accession into WTO, and the social transformation. Facing the adjustment of the industrial structure and the tense competition for employment, one needs to study so as to get an ideal job. Jobs with proper certification are the vogue today. Lawyers need certificates, so do accountants, and so do skilled workers. Even farmers who want to make big money need certificates. The "green certificate" that began in Daxing County of Beijing is getting popularized throughout the nation. Along with it, all kinds of training classes and foreign language classes have popped up and have become most popular. Many people have changed the long holiday periods of National Day and International Labor Day into days for study instead of sightseeing. One has to go at least six months ahead of time to register for foreign language classes at the New Oriental Foreign Language School. In China every citizen believes that they can get nowhere without knowledge and study. The Chinese people have entered the era of life-long learning, and have bid farewell to the idea that one's destination is set by just one form of education.

The development of vocational and technical education is the foundation of the structure of life-long education and an educated society. It is important to have schooling and obtain a certificate. What is more important is to continue to upgrade one's knowledge for more job opportunities. Therefore Chinese people must rely on the reality of China and establish an education system conducive to life-long learning. Schools should be further opened to society so as to play their role in diploma education, non-diploma education, continuing education, and vocational training. The contacts and channels among ordinary education, vocational education, adult education, and education for higher learning should be strengthened, so as to provide more opportunities for the education and training network at different levels.

(Written by Zhou Mansheng with drafts and materials from Gao Shuguo, Wang Yan, Ma Luting, Wang Ming, Wang Rui, Sun Hongtao and Yu Li)

Chapter 4 Quality of Life

Since the 1980s, China's economy has been developing at an annual average growth rate of 9 percent. This is an amazing speed and it has continued for twenty years running. By the end of 2000, the average GDP exceeded US $800 per capita. This marked the fact that China has obtained the second stage in its strategic goal, and generally speaking, the Chinese people are better off. The income for most of the Chinese people has indeed increased a great deal. The scale and degree of poverty has, at the same time, markedly decreased.

People's living conditions improved tremendously, but there remains the problem of psychological factors in acknowledging the improvement in the quality of life. In the realm of social science studies the terms "living standards" and "living quality" do not necessarily go together. This is because there is no inevitable relationship between the objective reality and subjective feelings. Good living conditions do not necessarily lead to a high degree of satisfaction. Studies by American scholars have shown that objective conditions only translate into 17 percent of subjective satisfaction. Therefore, a good feeling is indeed good.

1. Huge Increase in Income

Since the 1980s, China's economy has been developing

at a flying speed, with an annual average growth rate of 9 percent over the twenty years running. In the early 1980s, China set a goal of quadrupling the GDP by the end of the century. By 1995, China had already quadrupled the 1980 GDP. And by 1997, China had quadrupled the average GDP per capita. By the end of 2000, the average GDP exceeded US$800 per capita. This proved that China has obtained the second stage of its strategic goal, and generally speaking, the Chinese people were better off.

During the past twenty years, the income of the Chinese people has witnessed a big increase. In 1981, the average per capita income for urban dwellers was only 476 yuan, while for rural residents it was only 213 yuan.

One may ask, if the income increased, didn't the prices also go up? According to data compiled by the State Statistics Bureau, the index of the retail prices of commodities for the year 2000 was 356 if the year 1979 was counted as 100. As for the consumer price index, if that of urban residents in 1978 was taken as 100, than in the year 2000 it was 477; if that of the farmers in 1985 was taken as 100, it was 314 in the year 2000. The former saw an increase of 4.77 times in 23 years while the latter witnessed an increment of 3.14 times in 16 years.

In the final calculation, in twenty years, the speed of the income increase for urban residents and rural dwellers is about 3 times of that of the price increase. The average annual income per capita of urban residents actually shot up by 9 times while that of rural dwellers was about 7 times, excluding the price factors.

Along with the steady increase in incomes, the Chinese people have begun to accumulate their own assets, which was inconceivable twenty years ago. Of course, owning a house is one of the major ones.

By the end of 1999, the rate of private ownership of houses by urban families was 77 percent. At the same time, farmers showed greater enthusiasm in building their own houses. The investment in completed house construction in 1999 reached more than 200 billion yuan.

In respect to bank savings, people's enthusiasm for saving deposits never died down. Though the central bank has reduced interest rates 8 times since 1997 and levied taxes on interest dividends, by the end of May of 2002, the total savings deposits of the Chinese people exceeded 8,000 billion yuan. The figure for 1995 was only at nearly 3,000 billion yuan. Residents also increased their holdings of foreign currency deposits, stocks, bonds, and cash at an estimated 2,000 to 3,000 billion yuan.

In their leisure time a dozen years ago, people often gossiped among themselves about any farm family with 10,000 yuan in saving deposits. Such families were extolled and they felt honored and glorious. But now, even families with 100,000 yuan in saving deposits may feel shy about mentioning it.

2. The Scale and Degree of Poverty: Markedly Declined

In the late 1970s, China had just entered the new era of opening and reform, after the ten-year quagmire of the Cultural Revolution. As the Chinese people first had the chance to learn more about the rest of the world, they realized that how poor and backward they were.

At that time, China had a rural population of 250 million under absolute poverty. In the early 1980s, China's rural population living under poverty went down drastically, thanks to the policy of family contractual responsibility in production. In 1985, the poverty line was set at 200 yuan for an average annual income in the all-out drive to eliminate poverty. By then, there were still 125 million people living under the poverty line. By the end of the 1980s through the concerted efforts of the government and society, the population under the poverty line had been effectively cut to just 30 million.

In 1993, the government started a new program of poverty-elimination and upgraded the poverty line to 400 yuan. By that time, China had just 80.65 million people under the poverty line. During this poverty-relief drive, the line was adjusted several times. In 2000, it was set at 625 yuan. According to the government white paper *The Development of Poverty-relief in Rural China* issued in 2001, there were still 30 million people under the poverty line according to the 625-yuan standard.

The international community spoke highly of the successful experience China was having in its poverty relief efforts in the countryside, calling it "a great poverty-relief campaign."

Among the 30 million people under the poverty line, some are the handicapped who have lost their ability to work and receive social security protection. Some are farmers who live in areas with severe living and working conditions because of the lack of natural resources. Besides this, some are farmers who depend on the circumstances of nature and may become impoverished because of natural calamities. To these people living in poverty, the policy of social relief may be a more expedient choice. Recent years saw glad tidings in the establishment of a social security system for rural dwellers. By 2001, 14 provinces and autonomous regions had established the system, covering 3.13 billion farmers.

Since the 1990s, due to the drastic transformation to the market economy and enterprise reform, various economic and social contradictions came into being in China's urban society. A new urban group living in poverty began to take shape. This mainly consists of the unemployed and laid-off workers and their families. According to some experts, these involve approximately 15 to 20 million people.

Facing the eternal contradiction between efficiency and fairness, China had pursued a policy of "no ceiling for those at the top but protection for those at the bottom." With a view toward guaranteeing the basic necessities of daily life for the people, the government, in 1999, started an anti-poverty policy, namely to guarantee the basic necessities of life for the laid-off workers of the state-owned enterprises and to guarantee the delivery of pensions in the full amount to those retired from such enterprises. These are promises of income guarantees by the government to laid-off workers and to the retired.

In 1992, Shanghai started the reform of social relief in China. It is called a system to guarantee the minimum living standard, which means that the government will provide relief to urban residents whose average income per capita is below the minimum, thus ensuring that they will be able to maintain their families at the minimum, or subsistence, level.

In 1994, the Ministry of Civil Affairs popularized this system through a pilot project. And in 1997, the State Council worked out a general plan. By September 1999, all 668 cities and 1,638 county and town seats had established the system so as to ensure minimum living standards. In the meantime, on the 1st of October of the same year, the "Regulations to Ensure a Minimum Living Standard for Urban Workers" went into effect.

By the end of 2001 after two years of effort, the system had reached out to 12 million people. According to a news release by the Ministry of Civil Affairs, it was expected to cover 15 to 18 million people in the first half of 2002.

3. The Engel Indicator: Having Declined Dramatically

The international community attaches great importance to the Engel indicator of a country or a region. This serves as an important tool to measure and compare a country's income and living standard. The Engel indicator is based on the percentage of spending for food out of the total income or total spending of a family. By the end of the 19th century, Engel, a German statistician, had discovered that the lower the income of a family the larger proportion of its income was used for daily necessities; and the higher the income of a family, the smaller the portion of its income was used for daily necessities. This measurement is named "the Engel's law."

Later, the concept of "daily necessities" was replaced by "food consumption" in the United States, and the Engel indicator was used to draw the poverty line in the United States. Afterwards, the Food and Agriculture Organization of the United Nations set a general standard using the Engel Indicator to judge the development stage of each country's livelihood. If the scale goes above 60 percent, the country is said to be in poverty; between 50 to 60 percent, it is said to have sufficient food and clothing; between 40 to 50 percent, it is said to be well-off; and under 40 percent, to be affluent.

In the early 1980s, the Engel indicator for urban residents in China was 56.7 percent in 1981, and 61.89 percent for rural dwellers in 1980. These two figures were either close to or had passed the poverty line as measured by the Engel indicator. In 2000, the indicator went down to 39.2 percent for urban residents, passing through the threshold of affluence. It went down to 49.1 percent for rural dwellers, thus entering the stage of being well-off.

The drastic decline of the Engel indicator shows the remarkable changes that have occurred in the spending structure of Chinese families. They could now spend more money on more than just daily necessities. In terms of the residents' consumption spending, that for clothing and daily necessities went down while that for housing, health, education, entertainment, transportation, and telecommunications rose swiftly. The Chinese people are now turning from a life of sufficient food and clothing to that of a well-off and affluent life.

4. Upgrading of the "4 Big Pieces" of Family Possessions

Since the 1950s, the Chinese people have habitually used "4 big pieces" of durable consumer goods to measure a family's affluence and social standing.

From the 1950s to 1970s, the first generation of "4 big pieces" included bicycles, sewing machines, wristwatches, and radios. This set of desires lasted for thirty years unchanged. The items basically cost 100 yuan each. From the 1980s to the mid-90s, along with the continued improvement in living standards, the desired "4 big pieces" changed to "refrigerators, color television sets, washing machines, and tape recorders." People were thus pursuing goods that cost over 1,000 yuan each.

In the 1990s, the "4 bid pieces" again changed to "air-conditioners, computers, mobile phones, and cars." The consuming level of durable goods had been vastly upgraded. Some of those items cost over 10,000 yuan.

The State Statistics Bureau therefore decided that, as of January 2002, the consumer price index would be revised to include some of the major and expensive commodities such as cars, computers, and mobile phones.

Entering the new century, the consumption of families began to pass beyond the limited big pieces to include individual entertainment. Families focused on upgrading the quality of their food and clothing as far as daily necessities were concerned. As for durable goods such as color television sets, air-conditioners, mobile phones, and computers, people began chasing after new generation and better quality products and post-sales service.

According to data provided by the State Statistics Bureau, the six potential fields of consumption for development are as follows.

1. Consumption in housing. By 2000, 77 percent of urban families owned their own apartments or houses. In 2001, the sale of houses and apartments continued to increase by over 40 percent. Consumption in housing drove up the consumption in house furnishings, furniture, and electrical appliances.

2. Consumption of cars. By 2000, on average, one in every

200 urban families owned a private car. Car sales for 2001 increased by 20 percent and half of the total sale of cars went into the private sector.

3. Consumption of telecommunication and electronic products. Since 2002, the sale of these products has seen an average 20 percent increase every month.

4. Consumption of culture and education. The consumption of culture in 2001 was 80 billion yuan. The consumption capacity was estimated to be between 300 to 600 billion yuan.

5. Consumption in holidays and tourism.

6. Service consumption.

5. Consumption of Tourism and Holidays: a New Vogue

This story has appeared on the Internet. An American couple with five children was tight with their money. But during holidays, the whole family would go skiing. They had to buy seven sets of skiing equipment and clothing for their skiing. Besides this, they had to pay for transportation to the ski resort. Many people thought they were crazy. Later, all the children married but they always had fond memories of their childhood. They could never forget the happy days of skiing, even though they had led a simple life in childhood. Indeed, tourism is indispensable in family life in developed countries.

Before the drive of reform and opening up, tourism in China was almost solely a matter for foreign tourists. To the Chinese people, obtaining enough food and clothing were still big problems and there was no room to think about tourism and leisure. International experience shows that only when the income level rises to that of the well-off will people have a desire for tourism. Now that the income for Chinese urban residents has risen significantly, the Chinese people are at a stage of great expansion in their interest in tourism.

Along with the upgrading of their livelihood and the changes in their concept of life, tourism has become a new fashion for urban residents. During weekends, people go on outings or excursions in the suburbs or to scenic spots in the outskirts of the city. During May Day, National Day, or the Spring Festival, people are traveling. This has become a major way to spend the holidays.

Surveys show that in 2000 the average spending per capita on tourism by urban residents had reached 88 yuan and the total income on tourism had reached 451.9 billion yuan. Tourism accounted for 15 percent of the tertiary industry. Take the May Day holiday for example. In the seven days of the holiday period, there were 73.76 million tourists throughout the whole nation providing a tourism income of 28.8 billion yuan. Thus the term of "holiday economy" has come into vogue.

In the meantime, more and more Chinese were experiencing travel abroad. The income from Chinese tourists traveling abroad in 2000 was 13.56 million yuan. Just during the May Day holiday period in 2001, there were as many as 10,000 Chinese tourists traveling abroad.

According to reports in the foreign media, before the mid-1980s, Japanese tourists were often seen traveling in Europe and the United States; from the mid-1980s to mid-1990s, the tourist market in Europe and the United States received more tourists from China, mostly from Hong Kong and Taiwan. After the mid-1990s, more and more tourists from China's inland areas traveled in Europe and the United States.

6. Credit Consumption: Growing Among Urban Families

This story about "an old American grandmother and an old Chinese grandmother" has been passed around in China. The old American grandmother mortgaged her house when she was young and then took a job. She lived all her years comfortably in her house and paid back all her loans by the time of her retirement. The old Chinese grandmother desperately kept saving money from the very first day of work and managed to live simply most of her life. At the time of her retirement, she had saved enough money to buy her house.... This may be a self-mocking story invented by some Chinese who had a somewhat "vanguard" mind.

Indeed, the Chinese mentality on consumption tended to be "conservative," holding the value of "balanced income and spending" and that of "repairing the house before it rains," while holding a grudge against "eating and using all without reserve" and "eating this year's meal from next year's harvest of crops." This kind of consumption psychology made most Chinese unwilling to consume ahead of time and more unwilling to take "on debts." They thought more about the need of "safety in the future," and they were unwilling to spend tomorrow's earnings today. Thus, an effective demand could not take shape in the market.

Nevertheless, since the late 1990s, this conservative psychology and conduct of consumption has changed greatly. As of 1999, the Chinese government initiated a policy of individual consumption on credit and loans in order to expand the domestic demands. Individual consumption on credit and loans underwent its first breakthrough in the purchase of a home. The word "mortgage" borrowed from English has frequently appeared in the media in recent years. It is reported that in 2000 the total amount of loans in Beijing was 40 billion yuan, of which 30 billion yuan or 80 percent was for loans on houses. The total amount of loans in Shanghai was 42.7 billion yuan, of which 30.7 billion or 72 percent was for loans on houses. The figure in the central China city of Wuhan was 1.2 billion yuan, of which 0.5 billion yuan was for loans on houses.

According to surveys in big cities such as Beijing, Shanghai, and Guangzhou, about 80 percent of the interviewees favored credit and loans for consumption. It was found that 10 to 20 percent of them had experienced consumption through credit and loans. The interviewees used their loans for the following items, in order of priority, house and house furnishing, education, cars, major electrical home appliances, and daily necessities. Those with middle-level and low monthly incomes of under 3,000 yuan used their loans on various things such as housing, education, cars, furniture, medicine and health care, and daily necessities. Those with middle-level and high monthly incomes, above 3,000 yuan, focused their loans mainly on housing, cars, and education.

The media has revealed that since the commercial banks in Shanghai initiated loans on durable consumer goods in 1999, the total sales involved with loans exceeded 20 million yuan in 1999 and 2000. And so far in 2001, the figure is 6.3

million yuan used mostly for the purchase of computers and electrical appliances. In Guangzhou, over 40 percent of the purchases of computers was done through installment plans. Pianos and cameras were also among the items purchased through installment plans.

Nowadays, Chinese "credit" has become an invisible asset. One who wants to consume may obtain loans by his "credit" even though he does not have money or not enough money. This has had a great impact on the traditional concepts of the Chinese.

7. Continuing Enthusiasm for Consumption in Health

The Chinese saying goes this way, "One may possess nothing but money; one may have anything but ailment." This is becoming a common understanding in Chinese society. Along with the improvement in living standards, investment in health care is increasing. In 2000, the average spending per capita on health care and medicine for urban residents was 318 yuan, accounting for 6.4 percent of the total spending of a family, which was an increase of 189 percent over that in 1995. The breakdown was 76 percent for medicine, 13 percent for health care and services, and 6 percent for supplementary medicine. In 2000, the average spending per capita on health care and medicine for rural dwellers increased to 88 yuan, which was a 110 percent increase over that in 1995.

Since the 1950s, the average life expectancy for the Chinese people has extended continuously. A half century ago, the average life expectancy was only 35 years. By 2001, it had reached 71.8 years. In the early 1980s, the average life expectancy of the Chinese people was 67.8 years. In twenty years, four years have been added to the life expectancy. China is now one of the countries in the world that fits in the ranks of those with an average life expectancy above seventy years.

The extension of the average life expectancy of the Chinese people has resulted from the continued improvement of medical and health care facilities and the increase of the number of medical workers. In 2000, there were 324,700 health and medical institutions, while there were only 3,700 institutions in 1949. Even in 1980 there were only 180,000 institutions, an increase of 80 percent in twenty years. In 2000, there were 4.49 million medical workers while there were only 0.5 million in 1949. And in 1980 there were 2.8 million medical workers, an increase of 60 percent in twenty years.

China's successful bid for the Olympic Games has greatly pushed forward the drive toward keeping fit. It has become a way of life for many people to take part in sports and exercises in order to prevent disease. The aged get up early to do exercises in the parks. The young and middle aged go to gymnasiums after work. Children participate in various sports training classes. In 1995, China issued an "Outline for the Whole Nation to Keep Fit," which laid down the general goal of upgrading the physical condition of the whole nation. The requirements set forward were: exercise three times each week, with at least thirty minutes of exercise each session. A survey conducted in 1996 showed that one-third of the whole population often participated in sports and exercises. This compares with the 60 to 80 percent of the whole population participating in sports or exercises in developed countries. Thus China still lags far behind.

In the pursuit of good health, people are becoming more and more sensitive toward their surroundings and are setting high requirements. Surveys show that urban residents are quite satisfied with the changes in "convenience in transportation," the "green environment in their surroundings," and the "safe environment." The great majority believes that there have been great changes or some changes. In a ten-item survey they ranked those as the top three.

8. Continuous Increase in Consumption of Education

Based on an assessment of the trend toward developing knowledge and education, urban and rural residents have expressed an increasing need and demand for education. Education is a basic human right, and China has made great strides in pushing forward a 9-year compulsory education plan for 99 percent of the children eligible for schooling. On average, 621 middle school students and 1,076 primary school students out of 10,000 people are in school now, an increase of 174 and 5 students respectively over that in 1990. In 1999, 3 percent of the population had received education in higher learning institutions. Now there are 33 college students out of every 10,000 people. Illiteracy has been reduced by a large margin. The rate of adult literacy at the end of 1999 was 88 percent.

Besides this, education as an enterprise was brought into

full play. In 1999, the average amount of spending on education for every Chinese family was 1,014 yuan, 7 percent of the total annual consumer spending. Surveys showed that investment by Chinese families in education exceeded their spending on housing. In the education market, all kinds of training classes mushroomed for the benefit of quality education among primary and middle school students. Adults spent a great deal of time to "recharge" their knowledge. The expenditure on adult education in 2000 increased by 40 percent over that of 1999. On-the-job graduate study and adult college education also provided opportunities for urban and rural residents.

It became more and more common to find that self-sponsored students were going abroad for study. Surveys showed that 90 percent of the interviewees were keen for post-graduate study abroad. The fact that people were willing to invest in study abroad indicated that the Chinese people were able to accept the relevant fees as their income had increased on the one hand. On the other, overseas education was known to generate higher returns. At present, on average each year, 25,000 self-sponsored students are going abroad to study. If the annual cost was between 140,000 and 180,000 yuan per student, about 4 billion yuan was being spent for education abroad each year. There is also a tendency for more and more younger students to go abroad for study. In 1999, about 2,000 middle school students from Shenzhen went study abroad. Investigations showed that 1 billion yuan was being spent on primary and middle school students from Guangdong Province who were going abroad to study each year.

All in all, education as a part of the market has already opened but the boundary between education as a basic right for citizens and market operation seems unclear. Therefore, the developing trend for the future is hard to discern.

9. Social Classifications Beginning to Appear

Along with "letting some people get rich first," the gap in incomes is becoming wider. In 1997, the income of families in the top 20 percent was 3.1 times that of the bottom 20 percent, and it rose to 3.3 times in 1998, 3.4 times in 1999, and 3.6 times in 2000. The income of families in the top 10 percent was 4.2 times that of the bottom 10 percent in 1997, and it became 4.4 times in 1998, 4.6 times in 1999 and 5 times in 2000.

With respect to income, according to surveys by the State Statistics Bureau, the annual average family income above 10,191 yuan belonged to the group with the highest incomes. The income of this group has grown rapidly in recent years. Their problems in housing, medical care, and social security are basically solved, so that their consumption is stable and high. The group in the middle-income bracket had an income of between 4,316 to 10,190 yuan. The income of this group was basically stable, so that they had some surplus after they met the demands of daily consumption. The group in the low-income bracket had an annual family income of between 2,357 yuan and 4,315 yuan. They basically spent their money mainly on daily necessities.

The widening gap in incomes began to change the social structure. People of different professions or different incomes gradually evolved into different social groups. The past "pyramid-shape" of the social structure is now turning into one of a "spindle-shape." The group with high and middle incomes became the hot spot of the media. It was reported that they mainly included four categories of people: first, the traditional high and middle-income makers, or private businessmen; second, some managers of enterprises and intellectuals; third, private entrepreneurs (including farmer entrepreneurs); fourth, white-collar workers and professionals in foreign enterprises. This group accounted for 1 to 2 percent of the total employed persons in the cities. The development and growth of high and middle-income makers bears a positive significance in the shaping of an appropriate social structure, which is an important structural factor in social stability. This group is leading consumption and their way of life is an important guarantee to a stable consumer market.

Nevertheless, the emergence of this new generation of middle- and high-income earners was perhaps influenced by post-modernism, or maybe it just came into being and was yet immature. The media had the following comments about them. They attach importance to the quality of their own lives, pursue privacy and hold aloof from others, and do not want others to take too much of their time. They do not want to compete so as to be the first and neither do they want to shoulder responsibilities.

In the meantime, the Chinese people are conflicted about the widening of the gap between the rich and the poor. The result of a survey done in Beijing in 2001 was quite interesting. When asked the question "Do you think there should be a difference of incomes in a society?", 84 percent answered yes. But when asked the question of "how do you feel about the difference of income in your city or county?", 76 percent answered that the gap was too big. This reminds us that although people tend to acknowledge differences in income, their psychological acceptance of this fact is minimal.

10. Relatively High Degree of Satisfaction Among Urban and Rural Residents

Generally speaking, the Chinese people showed a positive attitude toward the changes in social and economic life since the reform. According to the data from a survey conducted by a survey company over a period of three years at the turn of the century, in 1999, 52.8 percent of the interviewees said they were "satisfied," or "relatively satisfied." In 2000, this was 55.5 percent, and in 2001, it reached 63.4 percent. The years of the turn of century witnessed a gradual increase of those expressing satisfaction. In 1999, 56.5 percent of the "highly optimistic group" felt the future was expected to "turn better" or to be "relatively better." In 2000, this was 63 percent, and in 2001, it was 56.5 percent. The sudden rise of 6.5 percent in 2000 might be attributed to the turn of the century when people were more optimistic. The attitude of the year of 2001 returned to the level of 1999.

The results of a survey in Beijing in 2001 echoed those of the above-mentioned one. When asked to make a judgment of the economic situation in the 1980s, the 1990s, and now, 31 percent, 63 percent, and 69 percent of the interviewees held a positive assessment. When asked to make a judgment of the social situation, 53 percent, 42 percent, and 50 percent respectively held a positive attitude. It was at a low ebb in the 1990s and now was turning back up to that in the 1980s. When asked to compare life in 1995 to that of today, 76 percent answered that it was either much better or a little better. When asked about whether his/her life will be better or worse in five years, 79 percent answered either much better or a bit better. The result of this survey showed that three quarters of those interviewed expressed a positive attitude toward their life now than that of five years ago and about four-fifths expected a better life five years from now. Hence, generally speaking, the assessment and expectation of the Chinese people's life was optimistic.

Nevertheless, because of the different interests of each group, different degrees of possession of capital, both economic and cultural, there are stronger and weaker groups in society. The interests of the weaker ones are vulnerable and they are powerless to protect them. So the state needs to come in to regulate them. In the survey in Beijing, when asked about the economic and social situation and the assessment and expectation of one's life, 10 percent, 20 percent, or even 30 percent voiced different opinions. When asked to make an assessment of the employment system and social security system and reforms of the different systems, 10 and 20 percent expressed a "loss." Particularly, over one-third felt losses in the medical care reform. This deserves special attention.

(Written by Tang Jun and Zhang Shifei)

Chapter 5 Social Security

The social security system is a "safety net" for society, and it is related to social stability and the balanced and healthy development of the economy. The market-oriented reform of the economic system has put forward a pressing demand for the establishment of a corresponding social security system. In the process of establishing the socialist market economy, China attaches great importance to the reform and establishment of the social security system and it has achieved great headway. China started the reform of the social security system in the 1980s. Since the mid- and late-1990s, China has furthered its achievements in this respect, with the setup of a new social security system, particularly in terms of a framework for a social insurance system.

As one of the most important social projects in the economic transformation and industrialization of the country with the largest population in the world, the reform and development of China's social security system still faces many difficulties and problems.

1. From Unit Security to Social Security

The social security system before the reform was one of a unit security system based on the economic units of state-ownership (township institution units, rural communes, and production brigades), with state financial support to ensure that there would be no bankruptcy of these economic units. It was operated in terms of cash, and no individuals had to directly pay fees for their security but enjoyed different benefits based on their social identity (office or factory worker, or farmer). The unit security system was a product of the planned economic system, closely related to the state-owned enterprises and a typical embodiment of the roles of the government and its enterprises. With the enterprises running society, a unit security system was required instead of a socialized social security system. After the implementation of reform and opening, the unit security system was recognized to be drifting farther away from meeting the needs of the competition and mobility of the labor force, and it was quite necessary to establish a social security system independent of the enterprises.

The new social security system is a socialized social security system. It should not only promote the transformation of each worker from being a "person of the unit" to one of being a "person of the society," but it should also be economically sustainable and be fair in coverage, level, and degree. Hence the new social security system should be changed from that of unit responsibility and total state financial responsibility. The funds should come from diversified sources instead of just one source. The benefits should be linked to contributions instead of one's "identity," and the system should strive for unity between rights and obligations, and between fairness and effectiveness. The goal of China's social security system, as clearly defined in the process of reform, is to establish a standard, socialized social security system that is independent of enterprises and institutions and has diversified financial resources.

With the above-mentioned goals in mind, China started the gradual reform of social insurance, social aid and social welfare, so as to promote the development of the new social security system. By the end of 2001, 108.02 million workers were covered by the basic pension and old age provisions, 54.71 million workers were covered by the basic medical care insurance, 103.55 million workers were covered by unemployment insurance, 34.55 million workers were covered by reproduction insurance, and 43.45 million workers were covered by labor protection insurance. That year the income and expenditures of the insurance fund were respectively 291.46 billion yuan and 259.1 billion yuan. The accumulative balance from previous years was 139.66 billion yuan. The expenditure on social aid and social welfare was 42.6 billion yuan, covering 15 million urban and rural residents who were at the minimal living standard. A total of 60 million residents were receiving temporary relief as were a great number of the handicapped, retarded, disabled, and others who were economically at risk.

2. Great Progress in the Reform of the Social Security System

China began the reform on social security system in the 1980s. Since the late 1990s, along with the deepening of the reform of the state-owned enterprises, the reform and development of the social security system accelerated. At present, a new social security system has been established, particularly one with the framework of an insurance system.

(1) The system of retirement pensions for urban workers went from a scattered system to one of unity. In 1997, the State Council issued a "Decision on the Establishment of a Unified Insurance System of Pensions for the Aged Workers of Enterprises" to give approval to the establishment of the system. In 1998, when the government was restructuring, the Ministry of Labor and Social Security was named as the administrative organization to run the social security system and local governments were given the task of overall management of the social security schemes of the industries.

(2) There was a gradual deepening of the reform of the urban medical care insurance system. This involved the insurer, the insured, medical institutions, and the medicine market traveling together along a twisted road leading to reform. In 1998, the State Council issued a "Decision on the Establishment of Medical Care Insurance for Urban Workers," which serves as the basic framework of the insurance system.

(3) There were strides made in the reform of unemployment insurance system. As in the economic transformation, the question of how to digest the large number of redundant "ineffective" workers by the millions in state-owned enterprises became a stumbling block that China had to overcome in the reform of the state-owned enterprises and marketization. During the 1980s, China started to set up an insurance system for the unemployed. Due to its narrow coverage and low rate of fund raising, it was difficult for the nation to shoulder the task. China had to find ways to fit the unemployment insurance system to the laid-off workers. Working through both channels was the way to ensure social stability in the process of marketization. In 1999, the State Council issued its "Regulations on Unemployment Insurance." The rate of the premiums for unemployment insurance increased,

insurance funds proportionately increased, and the fund scale expanded. As of 2001, China, step by step, had abolished the transitional "lay-off" system for urban and rural insurance and had merged it into the unemployment insurance system.

(4) With the establishment of the "combination of an overall social program with individual accounts," a social insurance system with Chinese characteristics was implemented. Within the framework of the basic pension system for the aged and the basic medical care insurance system for urban workers, individual accounts were opened, which is a component part of the two basic systems rather than a simple supplement. In the meantime, the system combined the current account of insurance funds with fund accumulation, which is a partial accumulation system of the management of "mixed accounts," or a mixed form. This is a new experiment in the history of the development of social security systems throughout the world. It faces difficult problems related to how to handle the relationship between the overall social program and the personal accounts.

(5) Great headway was made in the social aid system. The traditional social aid system mainly covered only those who were physically weak, who were disabled, who had no incomes, or had special difficulties. In 1993, the city of Shanghai was the first to set up a minimum poverty level for urban residents. This was later extended to residents in towns and rural areas. Faced with the huge population below the poverty level in rural areas, China now implemented an effective strategy for poverty-relief, which has since become an international example for solving the problems of poverty.

(6) The social welfare system is well under way, and it is a relatively high standard of social security. In recent years, the state on the one hand has increased the in-put toward

welfare for the handicapped, the lonely aged, the women and children, and other people who need aid. On the other, it has adhered to the principle of society running social welfare. It has changed its traditional practice of having the state take care of everything in social welfare by actively mobilizing all the forces of society and the market forces to help solve the problem of financial shortages and rigid mechanisms. Local governments have adhered to the principle of combining job-arrangement, support for job-hunters and self-employment. The practice of compulsory job-assignments for demobilized army men was gradually reformed to speed up employment of the demobilized army men. By developing a charity and welfare lottery, the financial resources for social welfare are expanded and the social relief work was put on a routine and standard track.

3. Taking Care of the Aged

The basic insurance system of pensions for the aged workers of urban enterprises was set up in line with the "Decision on the Establishment of a Unified Insurance System of Pensions for the Aged Workers of Enterprises." It combines the overall social program with personal accounts. It is a combination between the current accounts and fund accumulation. The purpose is, on the one hand, to meet the needs of the systematic transformation from "unit security" to "social security" so as to provide basic insurance for the retired without accumulated funds. On the other, in the hope of making the best use of the golden 20 to 30 years of economic growth and population changes, it is to help incumbent workers accumulate a certain amount of funds for their pensions so as to alleviate the burden of financing by the enterprises and to develop the capital market.

The mixed form has its own operational mechanism. First, it is a joint fund-raising system by both the enterprises and the employees. The new system stipulates that urban enterprises and their workers must fulfill the obligation of the payment of insurance premiums for the basic pension (self-employed and private businessmen are on their own). The ratio for the enterprises is generally around 20 percent of the total wage payment, while it is 8 percent of his wage for an individual worker. Second, it is a method for establishing an overall pension program and individual pension accounts. The basic pension consists of the base pension and the individual pension account. The base pension will be paid from the social funds of the overall pension program and the individual pension account can be inherited. Those who started to work before the new system went into effect would be given an additional transitional pension when they retire. Third, the new system requires the investment of the accumulated funds so as to add value to them. The overall social program should guarantee enough funds to give pensions to all the retired. In the meantime, it is important to reap returns from the investment with the accumulated funds of the individual accounts.

Through several years' efforts, the basic pension insurance system for urban workers has developed rapidly. A total of 86.71 million workers joined in the program in 1997 and this increased to 108.02 million in 2001. The pensioners increased from 25.35 million to 33.81 million. The income from the pension insurance funds increased from 196.5 billion yuan to 242.6 billion yuan. The average monthly pension increased from 430 yuan to 556 yuan. In the meantime, social service institutions (such as banks and post offices) were responsible for providing pensions.

Due to the large number of workers leaving the labor market and the rapid increase in the number of retirees, the premium rate for basic pensions was too high (as high as 28 percent). This imposed a heavy burden on the enterprises and influenced their participation in the program and the amount they provided to the funds. As a result, the income of the overall social pension program could not meet the expenditures because of the serious shortages in payments. If this goes on for long, it will have an impact on the sound operation of the pension insurance system.

In order to solve the problem of this imbalance in income and expenditures and the dwindling of individual accounts, the government, in 2000, put forward a new program to improve the system and designated Liaoning Province and several other provinces to select a pilot city in which to conduct the experimental program. The new program increased financial subsidies to the pension system and found new financial resources (the central finance alone gave 86.1 billion yuan of subsidies from 1998 to 2001). At the same time, it changed the ratio to 20 percent for the enterprises to provide to the overall social fund and 8 percent (increased from 4 percent) to be provided by the individual accounts.

4. The Multi-layer System of Pension Insurance

Supplementary pensions are an important component of the multi-layer pension security system. According to the foreign theory of "three pillars" for security of the aged, the basic pensions provided by the state are the "first pillar," the supplementary pensions provided by the work unit are the "second pillar" and those paid by the individuals the "third pillar." Since the 1980s, many countries have chosen the multi-layer economic security system for the aged as a policy to solve the overburden on state finances and to deal with the aging problem. In December of 1995, the Ministry of Labor issued the "Suggestions on the Establishment of a Supplementary Pension Insurance System by Enterprises," so as to put forth a framework in which develop a supplementary pension system by the enterprises. In December of 2000, in an "Outline of the Experiment to Improve the Urban Social Security System," the State Council changed the term of the supplementary pension insurance into an "annual fund of the enterprises." It clearly stipulated that the 4 percent of the total premium may be counted as cost and the annual funds by the enterprises may be managed and operated in line with market principles.

The supplementary pension insurance by the enterprises may be divided into two categories, an industrial annual fund and a local annual fund. The state encourages rather than forces the enterprises to establish annual funds. Limited by the management system and the capital market, the accumulated funds from the supplementary pension program lacked any channel to invest in the market so it could only be deposited in banks or increased through buying treasury bonds, the return on which is very low.

Commercial pension insurance is also known as a personal pension or a personal pension plan. As commercial pension insurance is purchased by individuals and families, this together with the public pension fund and the annual pension fund, make up the multi-layered pension insurance system. Along with aging, personal responsibility for the management of old age security is becoming increasingly important in pushing forward development since the 1970s. In the 1990s, China made great efforts in developing commercial life insurance. The total revenue from the life insurance premiums in 2000 increased by 20 times, among which life insurance saw an increase of 37 times. The further opening and sustained development of insurance after China's accession to the WTO will become an impetus for the transfer of savings deposits in banks to commercial life insurance. Therefore, commercial pension insurance has a bright future of development in China. The government should take the personal pension fund as the "third pillar" for the pension insurance system and promote it as a tax and investment policy.

5. The Staggering Reform in the Medical Care Insurance System

During the process of the reform of the market economy, the bulk of the state-owned and collective enterprises could not reimburse medical fees for a large number of workers because of business difficulties or the fact that they were facing bankruptcy, thus workers lost their medical security. In the meantime, many newly established enterprises, particularly the non-state-owned ones, did not have a corresponding medical security system. Besides, over demand and mismanagement stimulated some irrational spending on medicine, leading to the rise in the expenses for medical care. The increase in medical expenses exceeded the forgiveness of the national economy. Medical care has to deepen during the reform along with the deepening of the economic reform and enterprise reform.

The period from the early 1980s to 1988 was one of a spontaneous reform in medical care by enterprises and localities. The period from 1988 to 1997 was that of experiment in reform led by the Central Government. The Central Government issued its "Suggestions on the Experiment of an Overall Program on Workers' Medical Expenses in Case of Serious Ailments" and started pilot reform projects in southern China, in line with the principles of the third plenary session of the CPC 14th Central Committee held in 1993. Summing up the information from these pilot projects, the State Council, in 1998, issued a "Decision on the Establishment of a Basic Medical Insurance System for Workers." This set the basic framework for the new system.

The main features of the new system were low level (insurance coverage corresponding to the stage of economic development), wide coverage (covering all the work units in the urban areas and their employees), joint responsibilities (the work units and workers share joint responsibility for the medical care insurance fund), combination of the overall program and individual accounts (the overall program of the raising, management, and use of the basic medical insurance fund in combination with individual accounts). By the end of 2001, 90 percent of the municipalities at the prefecture level had started medical care insurance, with 54.71 million people having such insurance in 2001 as compared to 15.1 million people in 1998, and pension-earners from 3.69 million people to 18.15 people. In 2001, the national revenue of funds from medical insurance was 38.4 billion yuan while expenditures were 24.4 billion yuan, providing an accumulative surplus of 25.3 billion yuan.

Although the regions attached great importance to this work and made great efforts at it, the basic medical care insurance system covered just a small number of urban workers, around one quarter of the total number, a lower percentage than those covered by free medical care and the labor protection system in 1995. There were many factors involved in this. Objectively speaking, medical care insurance is called a "worldwide difficult issue" because it involves the relationship between the insured and the insurers and the complicated relations among the producers, providers, and circulators of medical service. Subjectively speaking, in comparison with free medical care and labor protection medical care, basic medical care insurance requires workers to pay a certain percentage of the fees (generally 2 percent of one's total wage) and it is good only for "basic ailments" and "basic medical care." And the percentage of reimbursement is not high. To the vast number of workers, this means that the benefits are lower than they were for the past medical care system. So workers who enjoy free medical care are not interested in the new system. There are still debates as to how to look at the function of the individual account, how to deal with the ratio between the two accounts, the criteria for payments, and how to define "basic medical care insurance," "supplementary medical care insurance," and "commercial medical care insurance." This influences the popularization of the new medical care insurance system to certain extent. Moreover, the differences in regions, industries, and the turnout of enterprises make the management even more difficult. Hence, how to further develop the basic medical care insurance system in urban areas remains an arduous task.

6. Will the Peak of Unemployment and Laid-off Workers End Safely?

Since the launch of the reform and opening up program, China has created 170 million jobs, but the situation of employment is still becoming increasingly serious. Since the mid-1990s, the number of registered unemployed in urban areas shot up, from 3.64 million in 1992 to 6.9 million in 2001 and the unemployment rate has risen to 3.6 percent from 2.3 percent. By 2002, the unemployment rate is expected to get as high as 4.5 percent. If the laid-off workers from the state-owned and non-state-owned enterprises are counted, there were about 20 million of them, or approximately 10 percent of the total business population in the cities and towns. This marked the fact that China has entered a new peak period of unemployment.

Under a market economy, unemployment is unavoidable. Since the 1980s, China has started to set up an unemployment insurance fund. According to the "Regulations on Insurance for Urban Unemployment" that was issued by the State Council in 1999, the fund for unemployment insurance comes from the work unit and the workers themselves — 2 percent of the total wages from the work unit and 1 percent of their wages from the individual workers. By the end of 2001, 103.55 million people had purchased an unemployment insurance policy, which provided an income of 18.7 billion yuan with expenditures of 15.7 billion yuan. A total of 4.69 million unemployed workers enjoyed benefits from this insurance and 3.12 million of the unemployed received subsidies.

The establishment and development of the unemployment insurance fund played a positive role in guaranteeing the basic necessities for laid-off and unemployed workers, promoting the reform of the economic system and the stateowned enterprises, maintaining social stability, and improving the social security system. Nevertheless, facing 10 percent of laid-off workers in cities and towns and a large number of potentially unemployed (the one-third redundant workers of state-owned enterprises and state institutions and the potential transfer of 150 to 200 million surplus rural workers to cities), 3 percent for the unemployment insurance fund is obviously too small. At present, China uses the registered unemployment rate as the controlling benchmark, which is now approaching the ceiling. Clearly the present unemployment insurance fund falls short in terms of being able to compensate all the unemployed and laid-off workers.

There are three approaches to solving the contradictions between the supply of insurance funds and the demand for unemployment security. The first is to increase the rate of collections for unemployment insurance, with the consequence of increasing the costs of labor. The second is to take various measures to open up re-employment channels so that there are more job opportunities and jobs. Because of technical advancements, it is quite difficult to keep a high rate of employment over a long period of time. The third is to upgrade the qualifications for receiving unemployment insurance while in the meantime lowering the criteria for compensation so as to reduce the actual expenses. At the moment, China has mainly adopted the last two approaches with some achievements. But in facing the big shortage of jobs during the 10th Five-year Plan period, urban areas may see the unemployment rate exceed the international alarming rate of 12 percent. To deal with the pressures of employment and unemployment, it is necessary to think ahead toward an adjustment in the revenue mechanism of the unemployment insurance fund, and to do research on the appropriate methods of payment and how the insurance is used. In the meantime, it is imperative to make great efforts to implement an active employment policy.

7. How to Give Farmers Security?

Since the launch of the program of restructuring, urbanization and urban reform have become a key to the national strategy of development, and naturally urban social security has become the core of the social security system. This does not mean that rural social security is unimportant, nor does it mean that the vast number of farmers do not need social security. In fact, since the late 1980s and early 1990s, China has encouraged and resumed the co-operative medical care service in rural areas and positively pushed forward the establishment of the pension and old age insurance system. The socialized pensions, old age insurance, and co-operative medical service have developed relatively fast in certain regions over time, but generally speaking the development has not been great with some halts in certain respects. The number of people who joined the rural pension and old age insurance program went down to 50 million in 2001 from 80 million in 1998. Rural co-operative medical services are still limited, and are mainly in the outskirts of metropolitan cities and developed coastal areas.

The halts and setbacks in rural pensions and old age insurance can be attributed to many factors, among which a major one has been different opinions on whether it is necessary or not to set up social pensions and old age insurance in rural areas. Those who were against it have offered the following argument: "Farmers are not capable or do not have the conditions to participate in pensions and old age insurance." They point out that rural families can still accommodate to old age, and so it is not necessary to go in for social pensions and old age insurance. The plot of land that a farm family has can serve as the last safety net for farmers. There is some truth to this argument but it should not be used as a reason for denying the needs of rural areas for social pensions and old age insurance. Those who are for such rural coverage give the following arguments. First, it is an objective demand resulting from the change in the social and economic structure and an important measure for dealing with the coming aging problem. Second, rural families face many challenges in old age. Along with the development of non-agricultural industries in the rural areas, mobile farmers, changes in family values, and the large number of rural laborers migrating to cities, more and more of the aged living in rural areas will have to live by themselves and will thus need the support of the social security system. Third, it is difficult for the rural persons of old age to entirely depend on farmland security. Though farmland has served as the last safety net for many centuries, its function should not be overestimated today because of the limits of the farmland system, farmland acreage, and the income from it. Simple dependence on it cannot maintain daily life. Fourth, those regions that have already had the conditions for it should be encouraged to continue the social pension and old age insurance program in rural areas in line with their own reality.

Co-operative medical care, free medical care, and labor protection medical care in the cities used to be the predominant three medical care systems. In the 1970s, co-operative medical care covered 90 percent of the administrative villages throughout the whole nation. Co-operative medical care and co-operative health care and a huge number of barefoot doctors were the three treasures that solved the medical problems in the countryside. They were honored by the World Bank and UNESCO as "the only model for solving health care expenses in developing countries." With the implementation of the family contractual responsibility system for production, the co-operative medical care system based on agricultural co-ops met setbacks. In 1985, co-operative medical care covered only 5 percent of the population. In the early 1990s, the only co-operative medical care that could be found was mainly in Shanghai and southern Jiangsu Province. With encouragement and pilot projects, the rural medical security program only covered 12 percent of the rural population in 1998. Although initial health care in the rural areas has made great headway in recent years, the lack of a co-operative medical care system has posed grave obstacles to the upgrading of farmers' health and to the social development of the rural economy. Almost 90 percent of farmers are responsible for their own medical expenses. This has hindered the development of the rural health care system as much as has the costs for farmers' health. It has made it harder to solve poverty problems (about 50 percent of poverty is caused by ailments and disease). Therefore, the question of how to establish a medical security system in rural areas under the market economy has became a major issue to which governments at various levels must turn their attention.

8. Improving the Last Safety Net of Life and Death

Social relief is the most fundamental element in the social security system, and is known as the last "safety net." The minimum living standard of security is a system of social relief aimed at the group living in poverty. Therefore, it is an important part and infrastructure of the social security system of the nation. It was the former traditional social relief system formed under the planned economy that was specially designed for "the disabled." Along with the deepening of the reform in the economic system and the emerging of a poverty group in urban areas, the traditional social relief system has found it difficult to solve the problem of basic necessities for a large number of urban dwellers living in poverty, particularly those unemployed and laid-off workers with the ability to work.

In 1993, Shanghai took the lead in experimenting with an urban social relief system by setting up a security system of minimum living standards. In 1996, the National People's Congress passed the 9th Five-year Plan that set the establishment of a security system of minimum living standards for urban residents as an important task. This promoted the development of the security system of minimum living standards. By 1999, all the cities and towns had established minimum living standards. In the same year, the Central Government issued its "Regulations on Security of Minimum Living Standards for Urban Residents" to provide the most basic security for urban residents. From 1996 to 2000, 2 million, 2.34 million, 2.66 million, 3.82 million, and 11.71 million urban residents respectively benefited from the minimum living standards. The finances came from the financial budget of the local people's governments. The local governments set the minimum living standards according to the necessary basic expenses of urban residents and families with an average income. Those with lower than the minimum standards could apply for subsidies. From 1997 to 2000, local governments put in 1.15 billion yuan, 1.2 billion yuan, 1.54 billion yuan and 2.96 billion yuan respectively. In 2001, the Central Government increased its funding for those with minimum living standards to 2.3 billion yuan to be obtained from the Central Government's finances.

The security system of minimum living standards in the cities effectively made up for the resolution of the poverty problem that the other social security system missed. It played its part as the last "safety net" and assumed an important role in promoting social fairness, maintaining social stability, and pushing forward social development.

The more arduous task is now to establish the social security system of minimum living standards for rural residents. Because of the huge rural population there are a large number of "three nos" (no income, no working ability, and no financial resources) who need social relief, as well as the 30 to 40 million rural population who live under the poverty level. To solve the poverty problems and lack of food and clothing for a large number in the rural population, China should continue to carry out the effective strategy of eliminating poverty. This is a positive policy in rural social security and the key to the establishment of a rural social relief system. Without developing programs and developing the economy in poor areas so as to eliminate poverty, pure dependence on social relief and a social security system of minimum standards of living will lay gigantic pressures on the national finance. Since 1997, localities with proper conditions began to phase in the social security system of minimum living standards in rural areas. By 2000, 3.002 million rural residents had subsidies from the social security system, and 3.38 million did by the end of May of 2002, which accounted for 10 percent of the total rural population under poverty. Along with the economic growth, the governments at various levels are attaching great importance to the rural poverty problem, and the rural social security system of minimum living standards has big room for development.

9. Continuous Development and Improvement of the Social Welfare System

Social welfare means that the government and society provide for the citizens' basic life security with a social policy and social security that continues to improve living conditions through various welfare services, welfare enterprises, and welfare subsidies. It includes national education welfare, housing welfare, professional welfare, social welfare for the aged, children and women's welfare, and welfare for the handicapped. The purpose is to improve and upgrade the quality of life of the citizens. Social relief is applied mainly to solve poverty and crises of existence problems for the unfortunate. Social security is mainly applied to solve the basic life security of workers. Besides solving the problems of the life security of some citizens, social welfare is used to satisfy the welfare service needs of all citizens. It is honored as a higher standard of social security.

The social welfare system in China mainly refers to the

system in which the government gives financial aid to the aged, orphans, and handicapped who have need of life security. With a view toward guaranteeing the right to live of these groups with special difficulties, the state has enacted laws, such as the Law of the People's Republic of China for the Protection of the Rights and Interests of the Aged, the Law of the People's Republic of China for the Protection of the Rights and Interests of Women, the Law of the People's Republic of China for the Protection of the Rights and Interests of the Handicapped, and the "Regulations on the Provision of Basic Needs for the Handicapped, Aged and Weaker Persons in Rural Areas.' By the end of 2001, governments at various levels ran a total of 3,327 welfare institutions that took care of 190,000 people. The collective ran 35,000 welfare institutions catering to 668,000 people. There were 934 privately-run welfare institutions taking care of 34,000 people. The government adopted a preferential policy toward the handicapped in running its welfare enterprises (38,000 enterprises in 2001). The policy required these enterprises to provide a certain percentage of employment for the handicapped, so as to help the handicapped who were fit to work with job opportunities. From 1996 to 2000, 1.1 million handicapped were trained and employed through government appropriations and security funds for the employment of the handicapped.

China also exercises a preferential arrangement. This refers to giving compensation and praise to those who have attained merit in the country and society. In order to protect their rights and interests, the state issued regulations such as the "Regulations on the Commendation of Revolutionary Martyrs," the "Regulations on Preferential Treatment for Army Men," and the "Regulations on Job Arrangements for Demobilized Soldiers Who Joined the Army from Cities and

Towns." These regulations include preferential treatment such as regular subsidies to family members of the martyrs, wounded army men, and veteran soldiers; universal subsidies to families of compulsory army men; waivers and deductions of medical charges for wounded soldiers; one-time offers of job arrangements or one-time economic subsidies for those who choose to be self-employed upon demobilization provided by the government for the demobilized army men who joined the army from cities and towns. In 2001, a total of 38.259 million people enjoyed the above-mentioned preferential treatments, including 4.506 million at the national level, with a financial expenditure of 3.25 billion yuan.

Social mutual aid is another non-governmental form of social security, which has developed under governmental encouragement in recent years. The Law of the People's Republic of China on Donation and Contribution to the Public, passed in 2000, gave legal standardization and encouragement to the regularization and systemization of social donation activities. The Central Government also enthusiastically encouraged governmental departments, institutions, and social groups to help and support families with difficulties in getting rid of poverty and becoming rich. Local governments provided aid and services to those in difficulty through community services.

10. Difficulties and Prospects for Social Security in China

Since the economic reform and with a view toward establishing a sound social security system corresponding to the socialist market economy, China has made rigorous experiments and practice in this respect. Up to now, China has set up an initial framework of a new type of social security system with multiple channels of financial resources and management. This framework, though still imperfect, faces many difficulties and challenges.

A practical difficulty is the pressure of the increasing number of payments from the social security fund. From 1990 to 2000, the number of retired employees of the whole nation increased from 23.01 million to 38.76 million, with an annual increase of 1.57 million. In the same period, the registered number of the urban unemployed and laid-off workers increased from 4 million to 12 million. The drastic increase in the number of the unemployed and laid-off workers has led to a dramatic increment of expenditure from the social security fund. The total national premium for welfare increased from 98.3 billion yuan in 1990 to 400 billion yuan in 2001, far surpassing the increase in the GDP and that of workers' wages. This rapid increment in the expenditures for the social security fund did not alleviate the burden of enterprises, but made the goal of "partial accumulation" of the new model of pension insurance void. Along with the intense aging problem, the pressure of "expenditure increments" in the social security fund increased. This poses as a serious problem for the continuity of the new type of social security system.

The Chinese pension and old age insurance system practices partial accumulation, with the aim of investing the accumulated fund for higher returns, lower payments, and the provision of more services for the old age security of retired persons in the future. The present practice of fund management and approaches can no longer meet the needs of "partial accumulation." Influenced by the sluggish economy and the big decrease in the interest rate of state treasury bonds, the returns from bank deposits and treasury bonds of the social insurance fund are quite low. The channels for market investment are not yet smooth and the system faces the difficulty of keeping and increasing its value. If the returns from investments are lower than the increases in wages and the inflation rate over a long period, the goal of partial accumulation will fall into a void.

The urban social security system faces long-term pressures as to how to "increase the volume" and "improve the system." The chief foundation of social security in the past twenty years has been the "Regulations" or "Decisions" issued by the State Council or local governments without a national "Social Security Law," "Social Relief Law," or "Social Insurance Law." The procrastination in developing legislation on social security failed to give sufficient authority to the new type of social security system and showed that the reform of social security lacked legal guidance. This resulted in difficulties involved in effectively implementing many reform measures.

The key work in improving the new social security system in the near future lies in progressing from the establishment of the framework to improving the system.

(Written by Wang Yanzhong)

Chapter 6 The Concept of Values and the State of Mind

In recent years, the Chinese people have experienced profound and gigantic social and psychological changes. If 1978, the year before and after the launching of the program for reform and opening up to the outside world, is taken as the watershed for comparison of the two, these changes will be easily seen. The general trend of changes in the social values held by the people demonstrate themselves in the following aspects: People's traditional ways of thinking have become more and more modern, which is in line with the process of the social development in China, and these changes will further advance the modernization of society.

However, it should be realized that the change from a traditional society to a modern one cannot be completed in one step and is bound to be a difficult process. Thus, it is going to take a long time to establish a new economic system, build a new social structure, form new cultural models, improve them, and bring them into play. In people's concepts of values, the mixture of traditional and modern outlooks is therefore a basic feature. Still further, the potential conflicts and tensions between the different concepts of value are unavoidable during certain historic periods of time. Difficulties in the transition from the old to the new concepts may result in psychological vacuums.

The traditional social psychology has been characterized as being closed-off, single-minded, narrow-minded, and dogmatic, while modern social psychology carries the features of being open, pluralistic, tolerant and active. The Chinese people are in a period of moving from a closed-off state of mind to an open state of mind, from a single-minded outlook to a pluralistic one, from a narrow-minded view to a tolerant one, and from a dogmatic stance to a flexible one.

1. Irresistible Temptations: the Reform and Opening up Program Stirs up the Era of a New State of Mind

Modernization is a process of comprehensive social changes that demonstrate themselves not only in the change in economic systems, social structures, and cultural models, but are also reflected in social psychology, directly and indirectly. Prematurely or belatedly, such changes are under the influence of social psychology.

Social psychology is an expression of people's knowledge of social life, sentiments, and intentions. On one hand, it is a weathervane of social change, and on the other, it is a barometer of the spirit of the times. From a unique angle, social psychology outlines the social spirit and atmosphere, reflects the effectiveness of social operational systems, and mirrors the strength of the adhesiveness of society. As the intermediary between social structures and social consciousness, social psychology can provide people with motivation and guidance in their social activities.

From 1949 up to now, the social development processes

in China have gone through two historical transitions. The first is symbolized by the 3rd Plenary Session of the 11th CPC Central Committee in 1978, when the period of "class struggle" was replaced by the era of "economic construction as the core." The second is symbolized by Deng Xiaoping's speeches made during his tour of south China in 1992 and the 14th National Party Congress, when the "planned economy" gave way to the "market economy."

Since the end of the 1970s, under the policy of opening up to the outside world and with the establishment of the socialist market economy, China has been engaged in a rapid transition from an agricultural society to an industrial one, from a rural society to an urban one, from a society of rituals and customs to one of law and reason. Modernization has been the theme of this era of social development. To be in line with this social development trend, social psychology has also gone through a series of great and thorough changes.

At the beginning of the 1990s, China's social psychology experienced another round of fundamental changes. Deng Xiaoping's speeches made during his inspection tour of south China marked another milestone for the emancipation of the Chinese people's ways of thinking. The thesis of "three favorables" (promotes the growth of the productive forces in a socialist society, increases the overall strength of the socialist state, and raises the people's living standards) broke certain ideological shackles that had prevented people from being creative and being more open to the reforms. It also offered new standards for judging progress and social development. The 14th National Congress of the CPC in 1992 set the goal of establishing a socialist market economic system so that a new round of reforms would unfold in China. This trend of social development and adoption of predominant social values have strongly guided the change and maturity of the social psychology in China.

As a logical result of the modernization drive, cultural change will pick up speed. Along with the switch from a planned economic system to that of a market economy, the arrival of a better-off society based on economic and social developments, along with a consumer culture that has hastily made its way into the people's daily lives, worldly concepts are unfolding in all aspects of society. In the overall situation, therefore, pop culture and common culture are expanding with increasing momentum, in comparison with the existing elite culture.

These economic, social and cultural developments no doubt have formed a strong background for the profound changes in the social psychology of China.

Psychological changes in society are influenced by major reform measures and the results of social policies. In turn, they considerably push forward social development. In the organic system of social psychology, values take the central position and exert a major impact on all other psychological aspects. The state of mind in society, however, is a direct reflection of the present social situation and the realities of life.

Since the introduction of the reform and opening up program, especially since Deng Xiaoping's speeches during his inspection tour of south China in 1992, the psychological changes have been characterized by the following aspects regarding the people's orientation toward values: they have been moving from more attention to ideals to more attention to realities, from an emphasis on obligations to an emphasis on their own interests, and from an emphasis on collectives to individuals. In the state of their minds, they have changed from being closed to being open, from passion to reason, and from a single way of thinking to pluralistic ways of thinking.

However, it can still be seen that when concepts and values change, this does not necessarily mean that people have completely dropped their former way of thinking and tilt to the current one in an extreme manner. To strike a balance between traditional and modern orientations is still a major characteristic in the people's concepts and values. While many superficial concepts have changed under the impact of the trends in life, some core concepts still maintain an important influence as a result of having been for a long period of time the keys to social culture.

On another level, the several key features of openness, pluralism, and reasoning shown by the social state of mind have brought about further effects: Openness has led to tolerance, pluralism has led to relativity, and reasoning has led to pragmatism.

2. Collectives vs. Individuals: When Big Rivers Run out of Water, Small Rivers Dry up

The relationship between the collective and the individual is a basic issue that everyone must face in their social life. For sometime in the past, a major characteristic in the leading concepts and values was the overarching emphasis on the interest of the collective to the neglect of the rational interests of the individual. Since the reform and opening up program was introduced, especially thanks to the development of the market economy, people have become more self-conscious and motives driven by their self-interest have become stronger. With regard to concepts and values that have occupied the central position, i.e., the interests between the collective and individuals, giving and taking, and the relationship between a given person and others, what is the social psychology today?

How can we interpret the interests between the collective and individuals? A survey that was conducted on how to deal with conflicts of interest between the collective and individuals indicated that 29.8 percent of the people chose that "The individual interest must be unconditionally subject to the collective interest," while 57.7 percent chose "to take the collective interest as the center and meanwhile look after the individual interest," 4.5 percent chose "to mainly take care of the individual interest and meanwhile look after the collective interest," 2.1 percent chose that "The collective interest must be unconditionally subordinate to individual interest," while 5.9 percent have said that it was still too hard to tell which was best. From this investigation, it can be inferred that the value of orientation on the collective interest is still recognized as important by the majority of the people. But we can also see that the value of individual interest has shown that the trend toward this orientation is rising.

How can people deal with the relationship between dedication and taking? The investigation has also revealed that the previously advocated values of "contributing only, no takings" is only appreciated by a minority of the people. "Less dedication, more takings" and "no dedication, but also takings" are values that are not encouraged in any society, but are ones mirrored only by a small number of people, while most of the people try to strike a balance between making a contribution and taking. The fact that "more contributing and more taking" is now chosen by a majority of the people indicates that people would like to realize their own individual values through working for the society.

In dealing with the relationship between self interest and those of others, people hold principles as follows: 44.9 percent of the people recognize the principle of "being beneficial for oneself, but not damaging the interests of others"; 32.5 percent agree with the attitude of "putting one's own interests after others and being happy to help others;" 21 percent favor "putting one's interests before those of others, while trying hard to look after others' interests"; and only 1.2 percent choose "to only take care his own interests, but not that of others." This investigation shows that the development of the market economy has wakened people's awareness of their own interests and strengthened the motives driven by their interests. The emphasis on rational self-interest has become an outstanding developmental trend in social values today. The majority of the people investigated, however, understand that stress on reasonable self-interest is not built on the precondition of harming the interests of others while "harming the interests of others in order to be beneficial to oneself" is not the choice of the majority. The mainstream social culture of "putting the interests of others first," which has always been advocated in the past, remains favorable to many people. A major change is that a fairly large percentage of the people have shown the tendency to strike a balance between the interests of others and themselves.

China has an old saying that goes: "When big rivers run out of water, small rivers dry up." When this saying was used to express the view that collective interests were more important than individual interests, the majority of the people studied agreed with it. This is also quite enlightening when we think about what effect will be brought forward by the tendency to increase the orientation toward individual interests.

3. Paver and Bill: Who Is More Respectable?

At the beginning of 2000, the TV series *How Steel Is Tempered* adapted from the internationally-famous book about the life of a heroic soldier, Paver Korchagin, who fought in defense of the young Soviet Union, aroused an enormous response among audience in China. Several mass media organizations opened columns to discuss the spirit of Paver Korchagin who used to be an idol for several generations of people in China, and also made comparisons between Paver Korchagin and Bill Gates, founder of Microsoft. These discussions focused on the values of the people today, especially the changes and the present status of their goals in life.

People made a great deal of unique and thorough comments on Paver Korchagin and Bill Gates. Although their views were not the same, there was one point in common. This was that both Korchagin and Gates were regarded as heroes. Korchagin was more likely regarded as an idol in the spiritual world and Gates as an example in the world of reality.

An investigation among university students in Beijing, conducted that year, indicated that when they were asked "Between Korchagin and Gates, who is the hero?" 44.9 percent of them chose both Korchagin and Gates; 20.4 percent chose Gates; and 17.5 percent chose Korchagin. With regard to the question who is your example of someone to be emulated, Korchagin or Gates, 44.2 percent of the people chose Gates, 27 percent chose both Korchagin and Gates; and 13 percent chose Korchagin. The youth had a tendency to choose Gates as their model because of the economic and social development and their own futures. However Korchagin inspires the people in today's world and his spirit is invigorating.

The ideals in the life of contemporary young people show an emphasis on both spiritual and material values. One investigation shows that the professions most admired by young people are, in the ranking from highest to the lowest: scientists, entrepreneurs, film and TV stars, army men, teachers, and model workers. However, for the most part, they want to become entrepreneurs, scientists, film and TV stars, teachers, army men, and model workers. It is clear that there is a difference between the professions admired and those chosen by the young people. In other words, the most admired profession is not the job that they would like the most. This reflects the fact that in their choice of professions, there is a difference between the value of ideals and the value of practical interests. They admire scientists most, but would most like to become entrepreneurs. Thus they are being more pragmatic in setting their life goals.

4. Post-workplace System: "Iron Rice Bowls" No More

The Beijing Morning Post reported on December 15, 2000, that the hi-tech enterprises at Zhongguancun in Beijing, called "Silicon Valley in China," had 100,000 university graduates working there without a permanent Beijing resident status. They had all found the jobs by themselves, though half of them who had been assigned to work in their hometowns had returned to Beijing, and another half had never left Beijing....

In the fully-planned socialist economic system before the introduction of the reform and opening up program, the issue of people choosing their own professions never existed because all the jobs were assigned to individuals by work units. From the very first day when one started working, he or she became a "person of the unit." The person's job, income, medical care, housing, entrance of their children into kindergartens, and their retirement were all tied to the workplace, resulting in a situation in which the unit had all the functions of a "small society."

Since the 1990s, the choice of jobs by individuals has gradually become a social reality and people have made more and more of their own decisions in choosing their professions. With the gradual disintegration of the "unit system," the government has introduced market-oriented employment policies. Especially under the great influence of the changes in social values, people today, particularly young people, have demonstrated diversified tendencies in choosing their professions:

First, in choosing their jobs, they have put more emphasis on tapping their own potential and realizing their own values. The first major consideration or standard for young people in choosing their professions is to see whether the occupation can provide them with a bright future for advancement. This shows that, as people have entered an economically well-off society, they no longer take jobs simply as a means for earning a living, but are more keenly aware of whether or not their personal goals can be realized.

Second, people have become more conscious of job risks in the wake of the gradual disappearance of the concept of "the iron rice bowl." In the past, people paid much attention to "job stability," but nowadays this is no longer a priority. "Realizing their own potential and value" and a "high income" have become major standards used in seeking jobs. The awareness of job risks, something necessary in a modern society, is gradually taking root.

Third, in choosing a workplace, the concept of belonging to a unit and getting paid by the government has drastically declined. With the establishment of the market economy, and the strengthening of self-consciousness, young people, in looking for jobs, tend to rely less on the unit and want less to become officials in comparison to the older generations. They now prefer to have more freedom and decision-making in their jobs, and would like to choose institutions more reflective of the times and more advanced in management.

Fourth, people are more concerned with being able to change their jobs at their own will. Changing jobs represents the fact that people have a greater degree of freedom in selecting their own jobs. There are signs that job changing is becoming more frequent and a great proportion of this job changing is the result of people making use of their freedom in selecting jobs. Most of the young people like to make their own decisions and rely on their own judgments when choosing jobs.

This type of job choosing psychology is rational. To begin with, it is a direct reflection of the growing complexity of the social structure and diversification of professions. Second, it is the result of pluralism and different outlooks. A clear example of this is the fact that there are a growing number of free lancers in the job market.

The fact that the book *Who Moved My Cheese* has been translated into Chinese and has become a bestseller sheds light on a simple truth called the "cheese philosophy": If somebody does not make changes on his own, he cannot adapt himself to a changing society and will finally lose out in competition. Changes mean the emerging of vitality and frequent changes denote pluralism.

"The cheese philosophy" seems to have become a unique footnote to the diversified psychological states of mind in people's choices for jobs these days.

5. Money: How Is It to Be Defined?

When the traditional outlook on values such as "gentlemen favor righteousness, while mean people favor personal gains" held sway, there was neither an economic nor a cultural basis for correctly dealing with the position and function of money. Therefore, emphasis on money was regarded as an expression of the seamy side of human nature, or at least it was linked with the week points in human nature.

China is turning from a traditional agricultural society characterized by pan-ethics to a modern society with emphasis on the rule of values. The speeding up of the market economy process and the deepening of traditional and conventional cultural developments have no doubt promoted the rise of a social environment in which money plays an increasingly prominent role. This development has provided the preconditions for the correct defining of the role of money, which is the most basic symbol of material interests.

People's attitude toward money can reflect, from a unique angle, their basic attitudes toward values, especially their basic state of mind with regard to social life.

Under market economic conditions, people tend to be more pragmatic in the orientation of their values. Material interests become an inevitable pursuit in people's daily lives. Under these circumstances then, what are the views and attitudes that the Chinese people hold today with regard to money?

An investigation indicates that 17.6 percent of the people studied consider the role of money to be "very important" and 56.4 percent "quite important"; 23.9 percent consider it "not very important"; and 2.1 percent think of it as being "not at all important." This means that the majority of people recognize the importance of money. At the same time, 24.7 and 24.3 percent of the people "do not completely appreciate" or "do not appreciate at all" the viewpoint that "Money is everything"; 28 percent hold a neutral attitude toward the matter; and only 8.1 and 14.9 percent are "completely" or "quite completely" in agreement with the view that money is the most important thing.

This is a new stage in people's values and state of mind since the introduction of reform and opening up program because the people not only no longer shy away from discussing money but they can even recognize the role of money. What is more praiseworthy is that while recognizing the role of money, quite a few of them have not exaggerated or over-emphasized the role of money. During the same period, the famous popular saying that "money does not mean everything, but without money there is nothing" has become widely accepted. This is no doubt a true reflection of the values placed on money, as stated above.

Although different groups of people have different attitudes towards money, the majority of them have the healthy state of mind that is necessary for modern society.

6. Love and Marriage: Let Love Dominate

The change in people's attitudes toward daily life has manifested itself in a most speedy and diversified fashion in the social psychology of China. Along with the progress of a more conventional society, people have become more and more open, tolerant, and rational in their attitudes on love, marriage, and giving birth to children.

In 2000, an investigation conducted among over 10,000 senior middle school students showed that 15.5 percent of them approved of premarital sex, and this attitude is higher among urban students than among rural ones and higher among boys than girls. At the same time 23 percent of the students approved courtship in middle school, and again the rate of approval was higher among boys than girls.

The same kind of investigation conducted among young people in Beijing showed that only a little over 30 percent of them were against the viewpoint that sex is acceptable during courtship even though it may not lead to marriage. The younger the respondents were, the higher the percentage of them in favor of this view, as there were 16 percent more among the respondents under 20 years of age who were in favor of this view than those over 30 years of age. From this it can be seen that the young people today are more open and tolerant in the matter of sex.

The investigation also indicated that young people are

clearly modern in their views on privacy, assets notarization, divorce, and dealing with the relationship of marriage. They paid great attention to the protection of privacy and even thought that the husband and wife should maintain their individual privacy. On the last point, 80 percent of the people approved and quite approved, while only 8 percent of the people held a negative attitude. Notarization of assets before marriage is a new phenomenon in social life and is also reasonably accepted by the majority. Over 70 percent of the young people thought that "It is in the interests of both the husband and wife to have their assets notarized before marriage." The investigation revealed that most of the young people could accept a divorce caused by the disaffection in the marital relationship, with 75 percent of them believing that divorce because of disaffection should not be condemned. Only less than 10 percent of the people studied were against this viewpoint.

As to the aspect of giving birth to children, women have also shown great psychological changes. An investigation completed in 2000 among female residents in large cities such as Beijing, Chengdu, Guangzhou, and Shanghai showed that near 20 percent of the people agreed with the point of view of having no children after marriage. And the approval rate was higher among young women than among middle-aged and old women, and higher among the women who had received intermediary or higher education than those who had received only a low-level of education. Meanwhile, the traditional concepts "of having children to look after the parents in their old age" and "more kids bringing greater happiness" have been gradually abandoned. The concept of "more kids bringing greater happiness" used to be a deep-rooted one among the Chinese people, particularly among

Chinese farming families. It was one of the concrete forms of expression most typical of traditional Chinese culture. To have more children has been a long-standing and difficult issue in rural China ever since the country adopted the policy of family planning in the 1970s. A survey conducted in the countryside in 2001 revealed that the concept of having a reasonable number of children or fewer children has gradually taken form within the farming population. The concept that "a family can be more prosperous with more children" is now only approved by 11.8 percent of the people, while 84.6 percent are against this, and another 3.6 percent hold a neutral view. It is obvious that the modern concept of reasonable fertility is clearly taking shape and gaining ground among the rural population.

7. Moral Status: Going Forward or Backward?

In the 1990s, shifts and the status quo in moral standards in a society undergoing drastic changes was the focus of much discussion, something people were concerned with and one in which it was difficult to reach a consensus. The academic community actively engaged in the debate over the differences between "moral decline" and "moral progress." Under the situation in which material interests are a great motivating force and commodity production and the rule of exchange have penetrated today's social life, is it still necessary to emphasize the role of morals, and if yes, how? How should one view the role of morals and the status quo today?

Using the proposition that "It is almost useless to uphold moral standards," an investigation team in the countryside, in

2001, found that 24.9 percent of the farmers agreed with this viewpoint; 11.7 percent of the people held a neutral attitude; while 63.4 percent did not support it at all. In other words, the majority of the people still thought that emphasis on morals was important in social life. As for the viewpoint that "One should act boldly where laws cannot be enforced," only 27.5 percent of the people agreed with this, 15 percent expressed a neutral attitude, and 57.5 percent did not support it. Most of the people put great emphasis on the special social significance of moral standards.

A very constructive example was an investigation among over 10,000 senior middle school students throughout the whole country that was conducted by the Department of Basic Education of the Ministry of Education in 2000. The study revealed that boys and girls still held in high regard examples of noble moral standards. The questionnaire asked: "Who is the person you appreciate or admire most?" The students were asked to freely write in the names of those they admired without being given any suggestions or clues. A total of 24.4 percent of them listed Zhou Enlai, who was ranked first by an overwhelming majority. The total votes cast for pop singers and movie stars were less than 20 percent. This indicates that boys and girls with strong self-consciousness and good judgment approve morally exemplary figures when listing their idols.

It is worthwhile to notice that in the era of replacing and rebuilding morals, traditional Chinese moral standards still vastly predominate among today's younger generations. The most typical example is that to respect parents is still the moral standard observed by most of the young people. An investigation in 1999 indicated that in regard to the degree of one's respect for and obedience to parents, 43 and 41.4

percent of the people thought that "they had done very well" or "quite well," 1.3 and 0.5 percent said "quite badly" and "very badly," while 13.7 percent said "just so so." Another typical example is that the concept of frugality is still recognized by quite a large proportion of the young people. According to one investigation conducted in 1997 of the viewpoint that "One should still lead a frugal life even when one is fairly well-off," 18.5 and 63.4 percent of the people expressed "full agreement" or "quite agree," and 2.4 percent opted to answer "difficult to tell." A total of 81.9 percent of the people still had not forgotten the traditional moral concept of frugality. Modernization does not mean a discarding of all traditions. To maintain the best elements of tradition and to carry these out in the new era is still quite important in the modernization drive. Young people have been demonstrating this quality in their actions.

It should be recognized that today's moral concepts embody certain conflicts and tensions. Unavoidably there are some omissions and disorders too. The emergence of new moral concepts is an inevitable demand of history and the logic of social development. Therefore the comment on either the decline or progress of morals is not a correct judgment or objective description of today's status in moral standards. In the world of great changes, the standards for the judgment of morals should be in line with the times. In reality, however, in making comments on morals, whether the comments are based on the past and are nostalgic-oriented, or based on the future and are future-oriented, people cannot reach the same conclusions. The theory of moral decline is over-pessimistic, while the theory of moral progress is over-optimistic. Either way, it will adversely affect the efforts made on the rebuilding of morals. Today, China should correctly tackle the question of new moral standards and qualities on the basis of the theory of the transition of morals.

8. The Internet Era: Facing New Uncertainties

There are more and more debates in mass media: Internet bars have become the most fashionable places of cultural consumption where the "new-new generation has come into being." Internet chat rooms are the places where people seek love outside their marriages. "The red-light districts" on the Internet have possibly become psychological traps for boys and girls. Internet articles have possibly infringed upon authors' intellectual properties. Today the Internet has become a sensitive area attracting much attention from different elements of society.

Since the second half of the 20th century, the Internet has been developing rapidly all over the whole world, enormously affecting the politics, economy, society, culture, etc. in all countries. The development level of the information network is one of the important indexes for measuring the level of modernization and comprehensive strength of a country. Hi-tech has not only changed the social structures and the ways of economic operation, but also people's psychological status and mode of action so that people's ways of living have also changed.

A report on the statistics of the country's Internet websites shows that up to June 30, 2002, China had 16.13 million computers hooked up with the Internet. The number of Internet users had reached 45.8 million.

Something called the Internet culture has come into being.

As a unique social phenomenon, the Internet culture profoundly reflects social changes and the rich status of social psychology. However, the network culture is like a "double-edged sword." If it is used correctly, the Internet can bring a great deal of efficiency and happiness to people, but if incorrectly used, it can bring negative effects and even cause danger.

On one hand, the Internet has opened a totally new cultural area for the people. There are virtual communities, e-commerce sites, information highways, distant education and e-mails. On the Internet people work, study, make enquiries, do shopping, chat, and play games. Each thing or every activity gives people a different kind of experience. On the other hand, while the network culture remains open to people's exchanges and mutual activities, it also contains the element of going-as-you-please and freedom, which causes challenges and difficulties in the legal and moral fields.

Among all kinds of Internet information, the biggest danger is different types of poisonous culture: first, "black culture" that holds a negative role in the ideological sphere; second, "porn culture" and "violence culture" that cause all kinds of negative effects to web users and can even lead to their committing crimes. Besides, "hackers" are quite harmful. Without obtaining authorization, hackers get onto computer information systems to make attacks, steal, tamper with, and delete information as well as using computer viruses to partially or completely damage the computer system. Thus it has become a serious criminal matter endangering the security and commercial secrets of the country and individual privacy.

Humankind has entered an information era that provides a totally new world. Therefore, in the control and management area beyond the traditional legal and moral spheres, it is necessary to immediately build and complete new network laws and moral principles.

9. High Expectations: Social Development to Which the Chinese People Have Long Looked Forward

To compare China with the earlier countries that started their modernization drive, China is among the third batch to begin the process. China's modernization program is referred to as a late-comer. The state of mind of the people in the late-comer category has one major characteristic, i.e., backwardness. People have a strong consciousness of the risks and a willingness to catch up and even to jump forward in great strides toward development. It should be said that this is normal.

To revitalize the backward nation in the modern time has been a great goal and aim that has been held by several generations of the Chinese people, who used to have a rich and civilized history. Young people today also have this frame of mind. One investigation conducted in 2000 on the social consciousness of young people in China, Japan, and Korea showed that the Chinese young people, compared with the youth from the other two nations, not only had a higher sense of national identity, but also had a strong consciousness that should contribute to the building of the country.

At the turning point of the old and new centuries, there appeared a new state of mind in the social psychology of the Chinese people at the same time that a "feeling of being at the end of the century" was circulating in some foreign countries.

Upon entering 2001, China played an attractive role in the world arena: having won the bid for the 2008 Olympic Games; having held the 21st University Games; with the National Football Team for the first time having entered the finals of the World Cup; having hosted the APEC conference, and having officially become a member of the WTO. Therefore, an American professor in sociology dubbed this meaningful year as the "China Year," which enormously raised the Chinese people's sense of national pride and saw a strengthening of expectations for national development and national revitalization in China's social psychology.

At the turn of the century, China realized the second-step target in its modernization strategy — to double the GDP and begin the march toward the third-step target. After the Ninth Five-year Plan (1996-2000), China bid goodbye to the economy of shortages and greeted the arrival of a well-off society. During the Tenth Five-year Plan period, more key modernization targets are to be realized.

An investigation carried out in 2000 among citizens in Beijing, Chengdu, Guangzhou and Shanghai showed that most of them were full of confidence in China's development in the new century. In the group aged 15 to 19, 68.8 percent said they were "highly confident," 33.4 percent were "very confident," and 35.4 percent were "quite confident." Among people aged 20 to 34, 64.7 percent showed high confidence, 26.1 percent were full of confidence, and 38.1 percent were quite confident.

China's accession to the WTO has led to an era of deep and all-rounded opening to the outside world. Meanwhile this era requires more and will create more talent to speed up the development of China. Indeed, an era that offers more opportunities than ever for people to set up businesses has arrived. This is an important reason for encouraging people to have high expectations about the future of the country as well as individuals.

10. The Future Trend: Emerging of a New Social Psychology

In recent years, the Chinese people have experienced profound and gigantic social and psychological changes. If 1978, the year before and after the launching of the program for reform and opening up to the outside world, is taken as the watershed for comparison of two different social development periods, these changes become even more obvious. The general trend of the changes in the social values held by the people demonstrates itself in the following aspects: People's traditional ways of thinking have turned more and more modern, which is in line with the process of the social development in China, and this change will further promote the modernization of society in the country.

However, it must be realized that the change from a traditional society to a modern one cannot be completed in one step and is bound to be a difficult process. Thus, it is going to take a long time to establish a new economic system, build a new social structure, form new cultural models, and improve them and bring them into play. In people's concepts of values, the mixture of traditional and modern outlooks is therefore a basic feature. Still further, the potential conflicts and tensions between different concepts of values are unavoidable during certain historic periods. Difficulties in the transition from the old to the new concepts may result in psychological vacuums.

Owing to the imbalance in economic, social, and cultural development, traditional forces and customs are likely to remain strong in relatively backward regions. Unsatisfactory aspects in the operation of the social system can also result in revealing the seamy side of the society. The limited abilities of some people and lack of confidence in changing the status quo may lead to a negative outlook and a backward state of mind.

An investigation conducted in the countryside in 2001 indicated that nearly 60 percent (58.5 percent) of the people approved of the viewpoint that "In real life, honesty suffers," 25.3 percent did not support this viewpoint, and another 16.1 percent took a neutral attitude. Obviously, quite a large percentage of the people had doubts about the value of honesty. This was a direct reflection of a credibility crisis in social psychology. In regard to the argument that "Money means everything and anything is possible with money," 61.2 percent of the people agreed; 30.9 percent did not agree, and 7.1 percent held a neutral attitude. This backward state of mind in believing in the huge role of money is in line with the economically backward situation that people are in. And this seems to be saying a lot.

Both negative concepts and the backward state of mind are temporary symptoms. Their positive role is that through the intermediary of social psychology, they have revealed problems that must be solved in the process of social development.

The accumulated results achieved in China's social development and the foreseeable targets to be realized have attracted people to the direction of progress. With the orderly and coordinated progress of the society and through the continuous explorations and trials of members of the society, a more reasonable, full-fledged and new system of values and state of mind in social psychology will gradually take shape.

Traditional social psychology is characterized as being closed-off, single-minded, narrow-minded, and dogmatic, while modern social psychology carries the features of being open, pluralistic, tolerant, and active. The Chinese people are in a period of moving from a closed-off state of mind to an open state of mind, from a single-minded state of mind to a pluralistic state of mind, from a narrow-minded one to a tolerant one, and from a dogmatic one to a flexible one.

However, when China has discarded some of the old-fashioned psychological outlooks, elements of the new type of social psychology required for future social development have yet to come into being. In this era in which the drastic changes have exceeded people's imaginations, a reasonable and future-oriented social psychology should be based on actual idealism and optimism in tackling problems. The completeness in human nature, the nurture of a sense of responsibility, education in credibility, and cultivation of sympathy and love should be stressed in the system of future-oriented values so as to promote mutual love between human beings and the harmonious co-existence between people and nature. This type of social psychology can be more compatible with the times and can better express an understanding of values and reflect more clearly human concerns.

(Written by Shen Jie)

Chapter 7 Science and Technology

Since the founding of the People's Republic of China in 1949, and especially since the introduction of the reform and opening up program some twenty years ago, remarkable achievements in scientific and technological development have shown that China is finally embarked on the road toward the center of world science and technology, after having remained away from the international scientific community for a long time. Professor C. N. Yang, Nobel Laureate in physics, clearly points out in his essay "The Entry of Modern Science into China: Past and Future" that "In the mid-21st century, it is very possible that China will become a powerful country in the world of science". But when comparing China with the advanced countries in the West, it can be seen that it is still backward in terms of scientific development. China's economic progress needs further support from scientific achievements. Some scholars believe that China is now still twenty to thirty years behind the advanced countries of the West in the general level of its science. China has actually caught up to some extent in science and technology, but the country is still only nearing the midpoint in terms of its technological level. Whether in terms of increasing the wealth of human knowledge or in satisfying the demands of social and economic development, science and technology in China still have a long way to go. The greatest risk for any nation is that it might have no sense of risks. China, time and again, lost opportunities for development in the wake of the industrial revolution. China will surely grasp the opportunities to develop and make new achievements in science and technology by mid-21st century.

1. Scientific Development Finally Has a System Guarantee

Perhaps among the leaders of the world those in China have the clearest understanding and pay the greatest attention to science and technology. Perhaps no leaders in other countries place as much hope on the development of science and technology as do those in China. Still for a long time in China there were no basic laws leading to the development of science and technology. Yet since the country embarked on the program of reform and opening to the outside world in 1978, the Chinese government has promulgated a series of important laws relating to science and technology and has made much progress in law making in this respect in the 1990s.

The Law of the People's Republic of China on Scientific and Technological Progress, adopted in July 1993, can be called the basic law for science and technology in China. It sets forth fairly completely the targets, role, source of finance, awarding system, etc. for the development of science and technology. It is a basic law guiding the development of science and technology into the future so that scientific and technological activities can be done within a legal framework.

In the ensuing years, there have been great increases not only in national treasury appropriations for science and technology but also in the total funds raised and actually spent on science and technology.

In 1993, the Central Government allocated 22.561 billion yuan of treasury appropriations for science and technology undertakings, and 1999 saw this increased to 54.39 billion yuan. During the same period, funds raised and actually spent for science and technology rose from 67.55 billion yuan and 62.28 billion yuan to 146.06 billion yuan and 128.49 billion yuan, both figures more than doubling the original allocations.

The R & D expenses for the whole country went up from 34.869 billion yuan in 1995 to 67.89 billion yuan in 1999, bringing up its ratio in the GDP from 0.6 percent to 0.83 percent.

Although this ratio was lower than that of major developed countries such as the United States and Japan, as well as that of South Korea and India, China's R & D spending was more than double that of India, nearly double that of Russia, and slightly lower than that of South Korea. The average annual per capita spending on R & D research increased from 46,000 yuan in 1995 to 82,600 in 1999. The continued increases of funding for science and technology have provided strong material guarantees for activities in scientific and technological development. In 2000, the total national R & D spending reached a record high, making up one percent of the GDP and ranking China first among the developing countries.

2. Explosive Growth in Scientific and Technological Human Resources

When the People's Republic of China was founded, there were only over 700 people working in the filed of science in the whole country. In 1960, the number reached 62,000 and in 1966, 292,000. During the ten years after 1966, the training of scientific staff bogged down. The human resources in science showed no increase. Instead there was even a decrease.

Since 1978, especially from the 1990s on, the Chinese scientific human resources have experienced an explosive growth. For example, in 2000 China had 1,041 different types of institutions of higher learning, 940,000 university graduates, and 301,000 post graduates out of which 572,000 majored in science and engineering, agriculture, and medicine. The number of scientific staff increased greatly from 506,000 in 1978 to 1.29 million in 1985, 2.5 million in 1995, 2.75 million in 1997, 2.91 million in 1999, out of which the number of scientists and engineers increased from 1.32 million in 1991 to 1.55 million in 1995 and 1.59 million in 1999.

Out of every 10,000 employers, the number of technical staff was only 869.5 in 1985. This figure, however, increased to 1,044.7 in 1990, 1,746.6 in 1995 and 2,748.3 in 2000.

Moreover, many young people are going abroad to undertake further studies in advanced scientific and technological knowledge in the West. Since the introduction of the program of reform and opening up, more than 400,000 young students have studied in advanced countries in Europe and North America, out of which over 100,000 have returned to China and become the backbones for different fields of science and technology.

Among these, Dr. Xiu Ruijuan used her own blood to conduct tests on artificial blood thrombosis and inhibition. In May 1984, "Zhongri," the first test tube sheep in the world, was created as a result of a research project by Dr. Xu Rigan and Professor Chen Zhangliang, vice president of Peking

University. This accomplishment has won many world-class awards. During the last twenty years, the number of students sent abroad has been more than at any other period in Chinese history and is also unprecedented in comparison with other countries in the world.

According to statistics, over 50 percent of the academicians in the Chinese Academy of Engineering are students who have returned from abroad during the last ten years or more. The same is true for two-thirds of the candidates of the "Across-century Advanced Talents Project," who have been strictly examined before being approved by experts of the Ministry of Education. This is also the case for the students who have returned from abroad during the last several years and are working in such projects and plans as "the Project of One Million Talents" launched by the Ministry of Personnel and six other ministries and committees, "Awards for Young Chinese Scientists" established by the Central Committee of the Communist Youth League, "Project of One Hundred People" set up by the Chinese Academy of Sciences, "Foundation for National Outstanding Youth in Science" and "Foundation for Outstanding Middle-aged and Young Talents" formed by the Committee of the National Natural Science Foundation, and major science projects including the "863 Plan" hosted by the Ministry of Science and Technology. The number of returned students from abroad in all these endeavors has reached more than 50 percent.

In 2001, there were 30.53 million members of technical staff working in different fields of state-owned organizations, which means that there were 2,734 members of technical staff out of every 10,000 employees; and there were 3.17 million people engaged in scientific activities. The number of those holding titles as scientists and engineers out of every

100 people engaged in scientific work increased to 66. This progress has further improved the structure of the technical staff.

3. Awards Bringing Greater Motive Force

As early as in 1955, the Chinese government promulgated its "Provisional Regulations on Bonuses for Science Issued by the Chinese Academy of Sciences." In accordance with the "Regulations of the People's Republic of China for Prizes and Awards for Scientific and Technological Progress" issued in 1984, the Chinese government set up prizes for scientific and technological progress, and established a working committee for giving national scientific and technological prizes. This marked the introduction of the scientific and technological prize-giving system.

The Law of the People's Republic of China on Scientific and Technological Progress promulgated in 1993 clearly stipulates that "The system of giving prizes in science and technology set up by the government is applicable to citizens and organizations that make great contributions." In 1994, the Chinese government set up China's prize for international cooperation in science and technology.

In May 1999, the State Council issued its "Regulations on Issuing the State Prize for Science and Technology" which stipulates that under the State Council the following prizes are issued: 1. Highest National Science and Technology Prize; 2. National Natural Science Prize; 3. National Technical Invention Prize; 4. National Science and Technology Progress Prize; and 5. China Prize for International Cooperation in Science and Technology. Meanwhile, the State Council spelled out conditions and procedures for the evaluation of applications for these prizes and the concrete measures for awarding the prizes.

On February 19, 2001, in accordance with the regulations, the Chinese government held a conference on the national science and technology prize in the Great Hall of the People. Under the admiring eyes of 10,000 people attending the function and amidst warm applause, Jiang Zemin, then President of China, handed out certificates of honor and bonuses to Professor Wu Wenjun and Professor Yuan Longping, two recipients of the Highest National Science and Technology Prize in the year of 2000.

From 1979 to 1999, national prizes were given for 12,582 scientific and technological achievements, out of which 632 were prizes for natural science, 2,973 for technical invention, and 8,977 for science and technological progress. Over 60,000 science personnel received national science awards and 20 foreign citizens obtained awards for international cooperation in science and technology.

Apart from the awards issued by the Central Government, local governments and non-governmental institutions have also set up prizes for science and technology. The year 1992 witnessed the Zhuhai municipal government giving large bonuses to people in science, with one million yuan each listed as one of the top ten news events in Chinese science circles during the year. Similar awards, such as the Ho Leung and Ho Lee Prize of the Foundation for Scientific and Technological Progress and the Yangtze River Scholars Plan have caught much attention from the Chinese scientific circles in recent years.

These science programs are characterized by awards given

directly to individuals but not to the units or organizations that have participated in science research projects so that the impetus is given to the people involved in scientific and technical activities. This way more achievements can be made.

The effect of these science award systems is not only beneficial to a nation and country, but also to the accumulation of science knowledge for all mankind.

4. Tackling Hard-nut Problems: from Catching up to Overtaking

For a long time, the Chinese government has launched different types of plans to develop science and technology. The "863 Plan," personally approved by Deng Xiaoping, was the first hi-tech research plan in China. Officially it is known as the "Outline Plan for Hi-tech Research and Development". In accordance with the principle of "selected targets and emphasis on key areas" and "aiming for frontline science," the plan called for organizing scientific staff to follow the world's advanced levels in the space industry, laser, biology, information technology, automation, energy, and new materials (two military and five civil fields), in order to narrow down the gap between China and the advanced countries and to make some breakthroughs.

From 1987 to 2000, the Chinese government allocations to the "863 Plan" rose from 12.5 billion yuan a year to 78.751 billion yuan a year, totaling 512.491 billion yuan. By 1998, 1,398 (49 percent) out of over 2,800 projects in seven major scientific areas under the "863 Plan" had been completed with achievements made. Among them, the accomplishments of 550 projects reached the international level; 495 projects had been put into application, and 133 had been commercialized. An official with the Ministry of Science and Technology has recently announced that "the follow-up approach" as a goal of the "863 Plan" has given way to "surpassing" or "overtaking" others in the scientific and technological area. The management system for the "863 Plan" has also changed with an expert management committee replacing the chief scientist.

The plan for tackling hard-nut problems in science and technology was by far China's biggest research aim in the 20th century, as stated when the program was launched in 1982. Its purpose is to solve key problems in the direction and general nature of national economic and social development. It is also a plan with the largest sum of investment in science and technology and the participation of the largest contingent of scientific and technological staff. On this more than one thousand research institutions and tens of thousands of researchers have put in their joint efforts.

During the Ninth Five-year Plan period, 5,100 special subjects in 251 programs were listed in the plan for tackling hard-nut problems. These covered agriculture, electronic information, energy, transportation, materials, exploration of natural resources, environmental protection, and medical care. For the plan, the Central Government put in 5.3 billion yuan and local governments invested an additional 17.6 billion yuan. Over 70,000 scientific personnel in 5,400 specialties from more than 1,000 research institutions and over 700 universities took part. Together they saw more than 20,000 achievements, registered 1,300 patented rights both in China and abroad, established 4,500 model bases for tests, and trained nearly 20,000 people in production experience and research abilities. In total, 430 billion yuan of general economic results and 95 billion yuan of direct economic results were generated.

The "Torch Plan," launched in 1988, is the most important hi-tech production scheme in China. Under this national guidance plan, a large number of hi-tech product development projects with advanced technical levels, enjoying both domestic and external markets and high economic benefits, have been conducted; a great number of hi-tech development zones have been established across the nation; and efforts looking toward a management and operation mechanism adapted to hi-tech development have been tried. The plan covers such key areas as new materials, biological technology, electronic information, integration of technology and mechanical and electrical products, new energy, and energy-saving technology.

By the end of 1998, under the "Torch Plan," 3,536 national projects and 9,036 local projects had been put into operation with loans from banks and funds the projects themselves had raised. In short, the plan employed the market economic system to finance itself. In 1998 alone, production output of the plan was 125.6 billion yuan with pre-tax profit of 21.2 billion yuan and export earnings of US $1.77 billion.

5. Market: the Key for Scientific and Technological Development

In order to push the development-oriented research institutions into the markets, the Ministry of Science and

Technology, the State Economic and Trade Commission, and ten other ministries or general administrations, with the approval of the State Council, jointly issued, in February 1999, "Stipulations on the Reform of the Management System of Research Institutions under the Ten General Administrations Supervised by the State Economic and Trade Commission." It was decided that the management system of 242 research institutions under the ten general administrations would be reformed in ways of their own choosing, including turning them into science enterprises, becoming partially or wholly merged with enterprises, or changing into technical service or intermediary entities. A small number of governmental research institutions approved by the government to retain their original nature as government-funded institutions should also introduce the operational system of science-oriented enterprises.

By the end of 2000, 242 research institutions had completed the system reform with 131 institutions having merged with enterprises, 40 having been turned into science enterprises, 18 remaining as governmental institutions but having changed into intermediary organizations, 24 being incorporated into universities or turning into other departments or being dismissed, and 12 (involving 29 institutions) having changed into large science enterprises directly under the Central Government. With these changes, 242 research institutions that were scattered in ten industries had completed the reform of changing their systems, which marked a major step in the restructuring of China's scientific research institutions. In 2000, another 134 technical and development research institutions managed by 11 ministries and commissions under the State Council turned into enterprises.

Meanwhile, over 2,000 applied scientific research institutions in the provinces had transformed themselves into enterprises by the end of 2000. As scientific research institutions were being transformed into enterprises, the reform in the welfare type of scientific research institutions that involved 360,000 people also began in 2001. This reform is now being conducted in 102 research institutions under four departments. During this process, many research institutions not only have successfully transformed their system, but have also given birth to a number of science companies listed on the stock market. The combination of knowledge and capital is closer than ever. Directors of research institutions have become board chairmen or managing directors and the market factor has been the key behind this change. Some experts believe that with the 242 research institutions under the Central Government being transformed into enterprises as a symbol, China's scientific and technological system has entered a new stage in moving from micro-reform to macro-reform, from system reform to structural readjustments, and from closed operations into open reorganization.

6. Space Project: Guarantee for National Security

China has a very long coastline and borders 12 neighboring countries. In modern Chinese history, the people had been subjected to great humiliations and had experienced many bitter memories such as the Opium War, the burning of the old Summer Palace, the Sino-Japanese War of 1894, and the Japanese invasion in the early 20th century. As a result, a strong national defense is of profound and direct significance. National security is a most serious object of pursuit of the Chinese people. A powerful national defense, however, can only be built on the basis of developed science and technology.

During the twenty years or more after the founding of the People's Republic of China, national security was under serious threat and the needs of national defense became the main driving force for scientific and technical development. Consequently, the Chinese government assigned a considerable number people and a considerable amount of materials to the development of science and technology for national defense with noticeable achievements. These have caught the world's attention. At present, China has nine models of Long March rockets capable of attaining low, medium-high, and high space orbits. The carrying ability of these rockets has been raised from 1.5 to 9.2 metric tons and the greatest carrying ability for the low orbit is 9.2 metric tons and for high orbit, five metric tons. The Long March rockets mean that Chinese space technology has a strong basis with the capability of sending rockets into different orbits and launching satellites with different weights, which are hi-tech products enjoying a relatively high reputation and credibility in the international space launching market.

China has also made great progress in man-made satellites. The country launched its first man-made satellite in 1970, and the second science experiment satellite in 1972. On November 16, 1975, China launched the first retrievable remote-sensing satellite, becoming the third country in the world with the technology to launch retrievable satellites. From 1970 to 1998, China launched three series of orbital satellites such as experimental satellites, communication satellites, and meteorological satellites. Altogether these totaled over fifty. Chinese scientists also had mastered the complicated technology of retrieving such satellites and synchronous earth satellites. Since China has had the technology for constructing nuclear bombs and hydrogen bombs, the country now also has the technology to put over fifty satellites into orbit.

Chinese scientists have been equally outstanding in the manned space industry, which is composed of seven major areas: astronauts; application of airships; manned airships; carrier rockets; space launching field; landing ground; and observations, control and communications. Since China started its manned space projects in 1992, over ten thousand people in more than 3,000 organizations throughout the country have participated in the research, construction, and experiments. During the last ten years, the technical staffs have carried forward the increasingly maturing space technology program, have opened up a road to manned space development with Chinese characteristics, have made breakthroughs in some key technological areas with intellectual properties, have upgraded the level of new sciences such as information, materials and energy, have improved manned space engineering with both advanced and practical features, and have trained a team of scientists consisting mainly of young people.

The year of 2000 witnessed China successfully launching the Shenzhou I and II spaceships, a development that put China only just behind the United States and Russia in terms of space exploration. On March 25, 2002, China again successfully launched the Shenzhou III spaceship from the Jiuquan Satellite Launching Center. The successful launching and return of Shenzhou III proved that China's man-carrying spaceship industry was maturing and it laid down solid ground for the launching of man-carrying spaceships. According to experts, the unmanned spaceship Shenzhou III met all the requirements for man-carrying spaceships. It proved that China had entered a new stage in the research in space science and resources through the use of spaceships, which was important to the development of science and national economic construction in China.

7. China's Contributions to Genetic Projects

The international human genome plan, dubbed a "moon landing plan" for human life, began in 1990 with the participation of scientists from the United States, Britain, Japan, Germany, and France. The core of the plan was to determine the structure of the DNA order, i.e., the analysis of the DNA elements of the human genome (nucleotide or base order) so as to lay the foundation for a survey technology of the human genome. In 1999, China became the only developing country to participate in this plan, responsible for surveying one percent of the human genome. The Human Genome Center of the Genetic Institute under the Chinese Academy of Sciences, located in District B of Konggang Industrial Park in Shunyi, Beijing, has taken on the task of the survey project.

Starting from zero, Chinese scientists within only two years completed their part of the task of surveying the genetic orders with high efficiency and quality. This achievement has attracted worldwide attention. The Genome Biology Information Center (namely, Beijing Huada Genetic Research

Center) under the Chinese Academy of Sciences, as one of the major research organizations that have completed the surveying of one percent of the human genome order, has become the 6th biggest genetic order survey center in the world. Chinese scientists have also made great contributions to the genetic order for plants. Twelve organizations have worked together on completing the "framework of the genome chart of long-grained non-glutinous rice," winning comments such as: "the most significant milestone in genetic research," "having forever changed research on botany," and "of great global effect to the health and existence of mankind in the new century." The organizations engaged in this research include the Beijing and Hangzhou Huada genetic research centers, also known as the Genome Information Center of the Chinese Academy of Sciences, China Genetic and Developmental Biology Research Institute, China Hybrid Rice R & D Center, and Washington University in the United States. A 14-page article in *Science* magazine introduced the main results of the research project achieved by Chinese experts, arousing extensive response internationally. The article has been downloaded more than 556 times from the Internet.

Furthermore, Chinese scientists have also achieved bumper harvests in medicine production and clinical diagnoses and treatments. As early as in 1988, Chinese scientists succeeded in developing vaccines for hepatitis B, and in 1992 they succeeded in producing a batch of synthetic artificial interferon, genetic medicines with special treatment results for hepatitis A and C. So far China has put 18 types of genetic medicines and vaccines into the markets. China is also advanced in the world in nurturing trans genetic fish, sheep, and pigs, as well as being advanced in the research on cloning pandas.

8. Hybrid Rice Defeating the Threat of Hunger

In 1973, Professor Yuan Longping, called the father of hybrid rice, was the first person in the world to develop long-grained non-glutinous rice plants with a three-line hybridization method. By using this method, he also developed many other types of rice. After the introduction of China's "863 Plan," the government asked the research team headed by Professor Yuan to use hi-tech to improve the quality of the agricultural crops and to raise the agricultural output. Yuan, in 1986, put forward his concept of a three-stage development plan for hybridizing rice.

With ten years of concerted cooperation and relentless effort by several hundred scientists in twenty-two institutions over the whole country, Yuan Longping finally succeeded in developing a new "two-line" hybrid rice, with an average output of 11,250 kilograms per hectare. The strain is the most high-yielding type of rice cultivated in large areas of farmland in China. On average, this strain of rice produces 100 kilograms per hectare each day during the period needed for its cultivation, from the sowing of seeds to the maturing of the crop. In 1990, the agricultural technology for this hybrid rice was transferred to the United States, where trial cultivation showed an increase of 38 percent more than the fine US strains in terms of unit yield. Now more than twenty countries, including the United States, Japan, and Brazil, have made use of this product. As a result, Yuan Longping has been awarded eight international prizes and is now dubbed the "father of hybrid rice." The progress and popularization of agricultural science and technology have enabled China to successfully use its 7 percent of the cultivated land in the world to feed its population which is 22 percent of the world's total. A professor from Purdue University in the United States has written that Mr. Yuan Longping has gained precious time for China. The increased production of grain he has brought about has actually decreased the growth rate of the population. He said that Yuan's achievements in agricultural science have defeated the threat of starvation. In his view, Mr. Yuan is leading people toward a better-fed world. Meanwhile, Yuan had also given a very meaningful lesson to conservationists on how to make achievements in agricultural science. Yuan has surpassed the West in becoming the first great scientist in the world to make use of hybrid rice.

The hybrid rice has made a great contribution toward solving the issues of hunger in the world. In 1981, the United Nations Food and Agricultural Organization and International Rice Research Institute set up a hybrid rice research center in Changsha, Hunan Province, where twelve sessions of training have been held on the hybridization of rice with some 200 agricultural technicians from 20 countries participating. In 1998, Viet Nam grew over 200,000 hectares of the hybrid rice and India grew over 100,000 hectares with an output increase of 1 to 2 tons per hectare compared to fine local varieties.

9. Great Benefit from International Exchanges

The opening up to the outside world initiated in 1978 symbolized China's return to the international scientific and technological arena. In fact, China's reform and opening up efforts first took place in the scientific arena.

During the last several years, Chinese leaders have paid great attention to international cooperation in science and technology during their contacts with foreign countries. From 1999 onward President Jiang Zemin put forward proposals at four unofficial meetings of APEC leaders suggesting the holding of ministerial level science conferences for the purpose of strengthening co-operation among the scientists and the industrial parks in the APEC member countries and regions, to draw up an agenda for science and technology cooperation in the 21st century, and to set up a foundation in China for science and technology cooperation among APEC members, much to the appreciation of the leaders from various member countries and regions.

In November 1996, President Jiang Zemin at a non-official meeting of APEC leaders made a proposal to strengthen co-operation among the science and industrial parks in each country. The State Council approved ten hi-tech development zones in Beijing, Suzhou, Hefei, Xi'an, Yantai, Shanghai, Shenzhen, Chengdu, Yangling, and Wuhan as science and industrial parks open to APEC. The Ministry of Science and Technology approved eight scientific undertaking service centers in Beijing, Suzhou, Chongqing, Tianjin, Wuhan, Shanghai, Chengdu, and Xi'an as experimental incubators for international enterprises to set up business and to build a network so as to promote internationalization in science.

During Jiang Zemin's visit to the United States in October 1997, China and the United States issued a joint statement affirming the achievements in scientific cooperation and developing exchanges between the two countries. They pointed out that they would further use science and technology to solve internal and international problems. Premier Zhu Rongji made a proposal at the Second Summit of Asian and European Countries to strengthen cooperation in science and technology. The Ministry of Science and Technology and the Ministry of Foreign Affairs hosted a science and technology conference of Asian and European science ministers in October 1999. The meeting adopted a "Ministerial Communique" and "the Chairman's Statement," which would exert a positive impact on economic and technical cooperation among the Asian and European countries in the 21st century.

According to statistics published by the Ministry of Science and Technology, China has conducted scientific exchanges with 152 countries and regions, out of which 96 countries have signed agreements on cooperation in science and technology or agreements on economic and trade with China. Within the framework of inter-governmental agreements on science and technology, different departments or ministries have also signed agreements on science and technology with the related departments or ministries of those countries. For example, the Ministry of Agriculture has established relations of scientific cooperation and exchanges with the agricultural departments in over 100 countries, the UN Food and Agricultural Organization and other international agricultural organizations. The ministry has signed agreements on cooperation in science and technology for agriculture with over twenty countries. The Ministry of Health has concluded agreements or memorandums on cooperation in health with 52 countries. The State Environmental Protection Administration has reached more than thirty bilateral agreements or memorandums on environmental protection with 27 countries. There have been extensive exchanges in non-governmental cooperation in science and technology. These exchanges are quite active among science institutions, universities, scientific academic institutions, enterprises, cities and scientists themselves.

For instance, the Chinese Academy of Sciences has built up relations of cooperation in science and technology with over sixty countries and regions and has signed more than seventy agreements of cooperation with academies in other countries and more than 700 agreements of cooperation with research institutions in foreign countries. The Chinese Science Association and its national academic committees have become members of more than 240 international science organizations. More than 280 scientists have held positions such as council members, executive council members or other leading posts in academic committees of international organizations in science and technology.

10. Greater International Competitiveness

There are many indexes to demonstrate a country's international prestige in science and technology. The US publication, *Science Citation Index* (*SCI* in short), is a very good means of measurement for basic research that reflects the number of results and quality of the Chinese scientists' achievements in this area. In five years, the number of papers from China carried by *SCI* increased from 9,927 in 1993 to 24,476 in 1999, an increase of more than 2.5 times. The proportion of scientific papers from China in the total number of papers carried by *SCI* also increased by more than 2.5 times. This lifted China from the 17th to the 10th top contributor of scientific papers in the world. It is estimated that in the next several years, it is possible that China's ranking in terms of the quantity of papers published in the *SCI* will still jump forward by one or two slots. This shows that the Chinese basic research ability has been strengthened. The result of its research has uplifted its world ranking and its influence in the world will gradually increase.

There are many indexes in the world that reflect the composite strength of science and technology of a country. At present, there are three journals that reflect the rise of China's international competitiveness in science and technology. The first is the "Report on International Competitiveness" released by Lausanne Management Institute in Switzerland, which sets forth the international competitiveness in science and technology of a given country according to 26 figures in 5 aspects such as R & D spending, number of R & D staff, technical management, scientific environment, and intellectual property. According to this journal issued in 2000, China occupied the 28th place among 47 countries evaluated in terms of its competitiveness in science and technology. In 2001, the journal adjusted its indexes, using the category of science infrastructure to match the science and technology index. It listed China's ranking as in the 26th place. The second is the "2001 Report on the Development of the Mankind" issued by the UN Development Program that reflects the achievements made by a country in creation, media technology, and training of people's technical skills. In its listing, China's technical achievements index is 0.299, placing it in the 45th place among 72 countries and regions that participated in the evaluations. The third is the "Report on International Competitiveness" published by the World Economic Forum. In this listing, according to indexes on creativeness, technical transfer, technology, and activation, China occupies the 34th, 43rd, 48th, and 47th places among the 59 economic entities evaluated. In short, China stands in the mid-upper level in terms of science development in the world, but there is still a large gap between China and the world's most advanced countries.

(Written by Wang Chunfa)

Chapter 8 Environment and Resources

More than 200 years ago, with the construction of the first steam engine in the United Kingdom, the great industrial revolution unfolded. Within less than 200 years, science and technology have developed by leaps and bounds, productivity has been greatly raised, and mankind has created enormous material wealth. At the same time, this progress has also brought about serious harm to the environment and a devastating consumption of resources.

Although large-scale industrialization in China has a history of only half a century, it has created serious problems to the environment and resources as a result of China's large population, fast development, and policy mistakes at certain times in the past. During the recent decade, the Chinese government and people have made relentless efforts in environmental protection and development. In 1996, China officially adopted the basic strategy of revitalizing the nation through science and education and of pursuing sustainable development. The last ten years are the decade in which China has paid the most attention and made largest investment in terms of environmental improvement. However, improving the environment is a complicated, accumulative, and long-term issue, which shows that protecting the environment and making a rational utilization of resources is going to be a long and arduous task. Along with the speedy economic development, the conflicts between population and resources, and the environment will become increasingly more intensive. People need to have a clear understanding of this situation and to make relentless efforts toward environmental improvement.

1. Awakening of the Awareness of Environmental Protection

About 4.6 billion years ago, the earth, our homeland, came into being in the vast expanse of space. In comparison with the rest of the universe, the earth seems like a spaceship cruising in the endless Milky Way along with the other members of our solar system. During the long process of evolution, continents and oceans have formed. At the beginning, the continent was a complete whole, called Pangea. Then 180 million years ago, the Pangea disintegrated and broke into separate continents and oceans. Some 60 million years ago, dinosaurs died out and the collision of the Indian Plate and Eurasian Plate gave rise to the Qinghai-Tibet Plateau, gradually laying the foundation for the eco-environment of today.

Humankind came into being only a little more than two million years ago, and most of the time human beings lived by hunting in a primitive society. The traditional agricultural society, which emerged during the New Stone Age, has a history of only a little over 10,000 years. The period of written records is only several thousand years. Because of the small population and low productivity during the long primitive and agricultural periods of society, human beings passively adapted themselves to nature. During this time, the relationship between humankind and nature was on the whole harmonious.

More than 200 years ago, with the first steam engine coming into being in the United Kingdom, the great industrial revolution unfolded. Within less than 200 years, science and technology have developed by leaps and bounds, productivity has been greatly raised, and humans have created enormous material wealth. At the same time, this progress has brought about serious harm to the environment and a devastating consumption of resources. This has led people to rethink of the consequences of development. As early as the 19th century, Malthus, the famous British economist, pointed out that excessive population growth would cause shortages of food, widespread contagious diseases, and war. Thanks to the development of science and technology, his predictions did not come true.

However, the problems of environmental pollution, brought about by speedy industrialization, have become more and more serious. Public dangers including death as a result of the carbon dioxide fog that appeared in London and Los Angeles and water pollution that occurred in Japan have sounded a warning to the people about environmental issues.

Rachel Carson's book *The Quiet Spring,* which was published forty years ago in the United States, listed a large number of alarming facts about environmental pollution. Ten years later the Roman Club issued a well-known report on the environment that reminded people of the limits of the earth in providing for the population of the world. On June 5, 1972, the United Nations for the first time held a conference on the human environment in Stockholm, Sweden. The theme was that "We have only one earth." The conference issued a

Declaration on the Human Environment that symbolized the fact that the whole world has awakened to the environmental issue. Within the next twenty years after that conference, people have made relentless explorations of the environment and developmental issues. In June 1992, the United Nations held a World Summit on Environment and Development at Rio de Janeiro, Brazil. This again clearly raised the issue of the sustainable development of mankind and issued *The Agenda for the 21st Century*. In July the same year, the Chinese government started to draft *The Chinese Agenda for the 21st Century,* completing the work earlier than was accomplished in other countries. The year 2002 was the 10th anniversary of the World Summit on Environment and Development in Rio de Janeiro. An Earth Summit on Environment and Development, the first of its kind, has just been held in Johannesburg, writing a new chapter for the history of civilization in human environment and development. The conference adopted *The Implementation Plan of World Leaders for Sustainable Development,* which proves that mankind has never shown greater concern for environmental issues than it has today.

Although large-scale industrialization in China has a history of only a half century, such industrialization has created serious problems to environment and resources as a result of China's large population, fast development, and policy mistakes at certain times in the past. During the recent decade, the Chinese government and people have made relentless efforts in environmental protection and development. In 1996, China officially adopted the basic strategy of revitalizing the nation through science and education and through pursuing sustainable development. During the last several years, the government has adopted a series of laws, policies, and regulations for environmental protection, especially focusing on the ecological environment in developing China's west. Many key projects such as the protection of natural forests, returning farmland to forestry, and controlling the sand storm problem in Beijing and Tianjin have been initiated. Measures have been taken to control environmental pollution, such as the treatment of wastewater in key water sources and the shutting down of fifteen types of seriously polluting small-size enterprises. It can be said that the last ten years are the decade when China has paid most attention and made the largest investment in environmental improvement. However, environmental control is a complicated, accumulative, and long-term issue. It is going to be a long and arduous task to protect the environment and make rational utilization of resources. Along with the speedy economic development, the conflicts in population, resources, and environment will become increasingly more intensive. People should have a clear understanding of this situation and make relentless efforts to improve the environment.

2. Once Again China Has a Blue Sky

During the last 200 years and more since the beginning of industrialization, 50 percent more carbon dioxide in accumulated exhaust has been released into the air and consequently the average temperature on the earth has risen by 0.6°C. The warming effect on the earth has led to more evaporation and more precipitation. As precipitation is not evenly distributed throughout the world, drought in the drought-stricken areas has become more severe, while in some other areas floods have become more frequent. Meanwhile, there have been more calamities of cyclones brought about by oceanic low pressure in tropical and subtropical areas. Developments of various kinds of refrigeration facilities and the great and long-term application of freon has led to a decrease of ozone in the air and a hole in the ozone layer over the South Pole.

China was very slow in embarking on its industrialization program and the accumulated hothouse air exhaustion is relatively less than that released by more developed countries. From this angle, the developed countries have more of a responsibility for the changes that have occurred in the weather. During the last twenty years or more, however, China's industrialization has quickened its pace, its fuel consumption has drastically increased, and its air pollution has become quite serious. The supervision studies by the State Environmental Protection Administration indicate that the major pollutants in the air are sulfur dioxide, smoke, and dust. In 2000, the exhaustion released by these pollutants was 19.95, 11.65, and 10.92 million tons respectively; and in 2001, it was 19.48, 10.59, and 9.91 million tons respectively. The statistics show that the figures for major pollutants were slightly lower in 2001 than in 2000, as sulfur had decreased by 2.4 percent, and smoke and dust by more than 9 percent. The total amount released, however, was still quite high. To improve the energy structure and raise air quality are very important tasks of environmental protection.

China's air pollution is mainly caused by the production of energy, mainly from coal smoke. Some 75 percent of China's energy is coal. Sulfur dioxide production excessively exceeds environmental standards and the acid rain problem has become more severe. More than half of the cities in the country, mainly those in the southern part of the country, suffer from acid rain.

In 2001, the air quality in one-third of the cities throughout the country reached above the second grade and in some cases up to the third grade. The major pollutant in the urban areas of China is inhalant particles, whose thickness exceeds the second grade national standards in nearly two-thirds of the cities in the country and the third grade national standards in nearly 30 percent of the cities. These cities are mainly located in the north and northwest of the country. This is related to the high consumption energy industries and desertification in these areas.

With the increase in the number of cars owned by Chinese families, gas consumption will drastically increase, and pollution in the urban areas will deteriorate the air quality because of the increase of such pollutants as nitrogen oxide and carbon monoxide. Therefore, China has adopted the strategy of developing electric vehicles and trains running on rails that should effectively reduce the amount of pollution being caused by transportation.

Urbanization has brought about an increase in population and the deterioration because of pollution. In order to solve the problem of energy pollution in the big cities, the government has made the "transporting gas from west to east" a key project in its strategy of developing the country's western region.

Some cities have made great efforts in reducing air pollution. The Chinese government has now clearly stated that the application of freon to refrigeration facilities is prohibited and a working agenda has been provided to improve the energy structure. In most of the cities, automobile exhaust has reached the Europe I standard, while even the Europe II standard has been reached in Beijing and some other cities. The fight against sandstorms in north China is already under way. It is believed that in the not too distant future the sky will become bluer and the air fresher.

3. Longing for Clear Water

China has a water resource of 2,800 billion cubic meters annually, ranking it the 6th in the world, but the country's per capita water resource is less than 2,200 cubic meters, only a quarter of the world's average. Furthermore, the distribution of water resources is by no means satisfactory. North China is home to 64 percent of all the country's farmland, but it has a water resource of less than 18 percent of the national total. The situation along and south of the reaches of the Yangtze River is clearly the opposite. At present, 20 percent of China's cities have difficulties in terms of water supply. The shortage in water supply is a common problem in northern cities. Because of the excessive exploitation of underground water resources in many cities, 56 funnel-like sink areas have been located with a total area of 87,000 square kilometers. Water resource has become one of the factors restricting industrial and agricultural development and urbanization in the North. Like surface water, underground water resources are rich in the south, but poor in the north. Taking up one-third of the area in China, the northwest of China has 112.5 billion cubic meters of natural underground water resources and 43 billion cubic meters of water is exploited annually, or one-eighth of China's national total. Furthermore, China is rather backward in the way water is consumed. The average water consumption per capita in China is 550 tons, 85 percent of which goes into agriculture. The effective irrigation rate, however, is only 25 to 40 percent. The water consumption in unit production is 5 to 10 times higher than that in developed countries. Thus the potential for water saving is still fairly large.

To alleviate the water shortage in the north, the government has started its plan to divert water from the Yangtze River to the north. While it is important to open up more resources, it is even more important to adopt the concept of saving water.

At the same time, China's water pollution is serious too. In 2000, the total industrial wastewater discharge was 19.4 billion tons with 4.5 billion tons failing to reach the discharge standard. Household wastewater in cities was 22.1 billion tons and the rate of treatment was low. Therefore, over 80 percent of the rivers in China have been polluted to some extent. According to the supervision and inspection of the water quality in 2001, the seven big water systems were seriously polluted. Less than 30 percent of the water was of good quality, meeting the first to third grade standards, less than 20 percent met the fourth grade standards, while more than 50 percent of the water was of the poor quality fifth grade and lower than fifth grade standard. Less than 50 percent of the water in major river systems belongs to the first to third grades. The water quality of the Yangtze River and Pearl River is fairly good, with 80 percent of the water in the Yangtze River reaching the standard for the second grade while 80 percent of the water in the Pearl River reaches the standard for the second and third grades. Soil erosion in the reaches of the Yangtze River, however, is deteriorating as the sand content in the water has increased, resulting in the worsening of the water quality. Large lakes in China are also severely polluted and the water quality of more than half of the lakes is of the fourth grade. Generally speaking, the water quality of large reservoirs is good, belonging to the second grade and a part of them belonging to the first grade and another part to the third grade. The government has launched large protection projects for the reaches of the Huaihe River and the Taihu Lake water systems in order to solve the water pollution problems there.

Now the water systems in the urban areas in China are also seriously polluted. Owing to the low rate of treatment for wastewater, many cities have not yet separated rainwater from wastewater and the wastewater is directly discharged into the rivers, resulting in a situation of black and stinking river water. Water in urban lakes has rich oxidation so that fish constantly die. People long for the return of clear water in urban lakes and rivers where birds sing and flowers blossom as was the case in the past.

The reasons for river and lake pollution are the runoff of agricultural pesticides and chemical fertilizers as well as pollution from urban life and industrial production. To upgrade the water quality, the traditional mode of agricultural production must be changed; organic fertilizer should be used and biological means should be adopted to control plant diseases and insect pests. Funds should be raised from all quarters of society to expand the building of wastewater treatment facilities in cities. In recent years, both the central and local governments and different areas of society have shown concern over the utilization of water resources and the control of water pollution. A plan for dealing with water pollution dubbed "China's clear water plan" is in the making.

4. Cleaning Away Garbage Surrounding Urban Areas

Industrialization and urbanization have brought about the concentration of the population and large-scale economy, but at the same time the costs to the environment are also very high. Everyday life and industrial production produce a huge amount of garbage. Due to the shortage of garbage treatment facilities, the treatment rate is low and consequently two-thirds of cities and most of the towns in China are surrounded by garbage. How to treat this garbage, turn it into useful materials, and beautify environment are major issues facing the local governments in cities and towns.

One source of garbage is solid waste matter from industries. The total industrial garbage produced is now over 800 million tons each year with an annual growth rate of 8 percent throughout the country. But more than 50 percent of the industrial solid waste is recycled. The annual discharge of solid waste from industries has been reduced to less than 30 million tons, mainly from coal, mining, metallurgical industries, and the chemical industry, especially from coal production that generates about a half of the solid waste. The accumulated industrial solid waste, totaling 7 billion tons, takes up a space of 700 square kilometers across the country. Some 5.8 billion tons of the solid waste from mining and related industries makes up 90 percent of the whole stockpile of solid waste. Cities with mining industries have more solid waste and the pollution there is severe. One-third of the large- and medium-sized cities in China are mining resource cities. As a result the pollution from solid industrial waste is a very serious problem. Many coal cities are full of piles of coal gangues forming a "unique view" of mining city landmarks.

Another source of garbage is produced by urban dwellers. Garbage now cleared out and transported away from urban areas in the country amounts to 150 million tons, nearly 6 times more than twenty years ago. This is mainly a result of the rapid urbanization process and the rise in people's living standards. In China, the harm-free treatment of garbage is less than 5 percent. The accumulated urban garbage is about 6.5 billion tons, occupying a total area of 600 square kilometers. Above two-thirds of the more than 600 Chinese cities are surrounded by garbage. The piling of untreated garbage around urban areas has polluted the water system, severely threatening people's health. And the white pollution from plastic garbage also has an adverse effect on the physical look of the cities. In ten to thirty years ahead, urbanization will further progress with a growth of 1 percent of the population. The annual increase of household garbage will reach 7 million tons if the average per capita garbage is 500 kilograms annually.

To separate household garbage according to classification, and especially separating recyclable metal, glass, plastic, and waste paper from other solvable organic matter will raise the quantity of garbage treatment and reduce the cost of garbage treatment.

In order to get rid of the garbage of solid wastes, the government has issued relative laws and plans. And some of the related technology is relatively mature. Industrial solid waste is mainly recycled for reuse or buried; urban household garbage is sorted and recycled for harm-free and resource treatment to produce organic fertilizers and building materials. Some cities in China have introduced or developed equipment for garbage treatment and have adopted a payment system for urban household garbage collection. Through the joint efforts of the whole society a more beautiful and clean urban environment will surely be created.

5. Converting Farmland for Forestry in Action

China has 7 percent of the land in the world with its major part located in the temperate and subtropical zones in the eastern section of the Eurasian continent. Varied natural conditions provide the basis for regional economies with different characteristics. The Qinghai-Tibet Plateau, Inner Mongolia Plateau, and the northwest region constitute the production base for animal husbandry. The hilly middle section provides favorable conditions for forestry. The northeast, north, and reaches of the Yangtze River form the agricultural base. The coastal areas are the bases for aquatic products. However, as two-thirds of China's land is mountainous, the ecological environment is very delicate and soil and water erosion is quite serious.

At present, the areas suffering from soil and water erosion occupy 16.7 percent of the country's total landmass and the total soil and water erosion amounts to 4.6 billion tons, mainly in the upper reaches of the Xiliao River, Yellow Loess Plateau, middle and lower reaches of the Jialing River, lower reaches of the Jinsha River, the Hengduan Mountains, and the karst regions in China's southwest.

China is proud of the Qinghai-Tibet Plateau, known as the Roof of the World. It is the home of the source of the Yellow River, Yangtze River, and Lancang River, the last of which flows on into neighboring countries. So the plateau has been fondly referred to as the "source of three rivers." Water and soil erosion as a result of ecological damage and vegetation degeneration, however, poses a serious threat to the source of the three rivers. The floods in the reaches of the Yangtze River in 1998 were caused by natural meteorological forces, but also had something to do with the reduced ability of the soil and water conservation and the weakening of the flood combating ability along the Yangtze River. During the last fifty years and more, forest coverage in the upper reaches of the Yangtze River has been reduced from 30 percent to 15 percent of the area, causing the deterioration of soil erosion. The average sand content at Yichang is 1.3 kilogram per cubic meter of water, and a total of about 600 million tons of sand is carried away by the water in the Yangtze annually. Therefore, if water and soil erosion in the upper reaches of the Yangtze River is not held in check immediately, there is the risk that the Yangtze River will become as muddy as the Yellow River. The government has taken measures to introduce protection projects of natural forests in the upper reaches of the Yangtze River and the Yellow River so as to effectively control water and the soil erosion problems in the upper reaches of these large rivers.

Water and soil erosion causes rock deserts. Rock deserts, mainly located in the karst areas of southwest China, are expanding at a speed of 2,500 square kilometers per year. Their harm is no less serious than desertification. The Yellow Loess Plateau is a natural environment rarely seen in other parts of the world. However, water and soil erosion is serious there too. The riverbeds of the rivers in the middle and lower reaches of the Yellow River have been constantly silted up and raised so that they have become "hanging rivers on the earth." Areas hit by water and soil erosion in the Yellow

Loess Plateau cover 500,000 square kilometers, of which more than 50 percent is severely affected. Specifically, 20 percent of the areas see the loss of more than 10,000 tons per square kilometer annually. Every year, 800 million tons of mud and sand flow into the Yellow River with a loss of 5 million tons of nutrients such as nitrogen, phosphorus, and potassium. The cause of this soil erosion is the thinning of vegetation in mountainous areas. Today China's forests are less than 2 *mu* (One *mu* equals one-sixth of an acre or one-fifteenth of a hectare) per capita and accumulative timber is only 9 cubic meters per capita. With the efforts made in recent years, China's forest coverage rate has reached 16.5 percent, but the forest coverage is still too low in many areas. In the northwest, for example, the rate is only 5 percent, much lower than the world's average of 27 percent. However, compared with 8.6 percent in the 1950s, the figure of 16.5 percent shows much progress.

In order to increase the vegetation coverage in the mountainous areas and reduce soil erosion in China's west, the government has started a project to convert farmland into forestry during its program of developing the west. This gives hope to holding water and soil erosion in check.

6. Controlling Desertification and Sandstorms

Desertification is a difficult ecological challenge facing the world today. China is one of the countries suffering most seriously from desertification, where sandy areas take up about 18 percent of the land total. Desertification refers to the process in which the land turns sandy or into a desert, but there is a great difference between sandy land and a desert. Sandy land refers to sandy farmland where plants can still grow, or to land for forests or grass, while a desert refers to land with little vegetation, where plants can hardly survive. Usually, a desert is formed in the paleo-geological ages. It is generally sandy land, not natural deserts, that gives rise to sandstorms.

China's sandy land and deserts are located in the eastern part of the Central Asian Desert, one of the four largest deserts in the world. The area of deserts, Gobi land, and barren sandy land in China occupies 1.7 million square kilometers of the national territory.

In recent years, China's desertification and sandstorms have been getting increasingly serious. The average areas turning to desert were 1,560 square kilometers annually in the 1950s and 1960s. This rose to 2,100 square kilometers in the 1970s and 1980s, 2,460 square kilometers in the mid-1990s, and now to 3,436 square kilometers a year. Each year new desert takes away an area equivalent to the territory of a medium-sized county, causing a direct loss of over 50 billion yuan. More seriously, this desertification causes more frequent sandstorms. Not only is Beijing hit by sandstorms but most of the cities in north China, including Xian and Shenyang, are attacked. In the spring of recent years, sandstorms also have affected southern cities such as Nanjing and Shanghai. In the past, the sandstorm weather occurs mainly in the spring, but now even in winter there are sandstorms. In some areas in the winter of 2001, the "yellow snow" that descended was an example of winter sandstorms.

Desertification and sandstorms are due to two factors. The first is natural causes. Especially in recent years, the appearance of La Nina weather and the release of greenhouse gases have led to the warming up of the global weather and constant drought. The second is irrational human economic and social activities, such as excessive farming, grazing on pastureland, mining, lumbering, and abusing of water resources. The desertification process is induced by man's activities and worsened by a complementary effect of natural and human factors.

In over fifty years since the founding of the People's Republic of China, the government has carried out several campaigns against desertification. Especially during the last decade, the government has paid great attention to the prevention of desertification in north China, initiating a series of projects such as the shelter forests in the north, northeast, and northwest of China; a sand control project; a program for converting farmland back to forestry and pastureland, and the sand control project in Beijing and Tianjin. Limited by economic resources in the past, the investment in anti-desertification projects each year was small, resulting in slow progress in the controlling of desertification. The control strategy was inappropriate, there were technical errors, the role of the sandy areas was not properly defined, the issues of existence and development of local farmers and herdsmen were not fundamentally solved so that excessive farming and pasturing could not be controlled, and the destruction and degeneration of forest and pastureland outdid the speed of sand control. All of these matters led to the situation of "no trees can be seen though planting is done every year," and "partial control of desertification is met only by total deterioration." In order to learn lessons from the past, single-minded afforestation has given way to plans for promoting sustainable growth of the local economy in fighting desertification. A strategy that combines desertification control and prevention with an emphasis on the latter has been introduced. One-sided fighting against desertification has been gradually replaced by efforts to give equal emphasis to the fight against sand and poverty.

Sand control is not only related to the existence and development of the local economy, but also to the ecological security in north China. Funding for sand control in the future, therefore, will mostly come from the Central Government, with backup from authorities in the benefited areas, sandy areas, and from contributions by the society as a whole as well as the international community. All the beneficiary cities and areas should support each other. As in the case of relocating migrants for the Three Gorges Project, it is of great importance to help settle migrants in the sandy areas.

7. Protecting Homeless Creatures

Due to environmental pollution and ecological damages ever since the industrialization, biological species on the earth have become extinct nearly a thousand times faster than they would have by the natural extinction process. Every year nearly a thousand species disappear from the earth. About 1.7 million species have been recognized around the globe but many became extinct even before they are discovered. Food and many medicines for human beings are based on biological resources. The reduction of biological varieties is the biggest resource loss for mankind and will increase the fragility of man's living environment.

Forests are major places for wildlife. Forest coverage on

the earth 150 years ago was 37 percent, but this has now been reduced by 10 percent. Especially rain forests, regarded as "the lungs of the earth," have been reduced by almost half. Every year 100,000 square kilometers of forest have been cut down for lumber. Since most countries in Africa, Asia, and Latin America are economically poor and where modes of production are underdeveloped, excessive felling of trees in the rain forests in these areas is difficult to stop. Destructive lumbering in the rain forests along the Amazon River is so serious that there are risks that the rain forests may disappear. As the global ecological environment is a whole, this shrinking of rain forests will not only weaken absorption of greenhouse gases, such as carbon dioxide, but it will also cause an increase in the global temperature and weather changes. More severely, it may take away their best homeland from wild animals and plants and, through the biological chain, lead to a series of biological extinctions and variety reductions. The disappearance of the rain forests, therefore, will be the worst ecological disaster for humankind.

China is rich in resources of species. The country's major wildlife, such as mammals and birds, make up more than 10 percent of all species in the world, with fish, algae, pteridophytes, and gymnosperms making up 20 to 30 percent of the total of these species in the world. China has various natural environmental conditions from the torrid zone to the frigid and temperate zone and the highland polar frigid zone, providing different types of living things with an expansive living space. China's southwest is reputed to be the "kingdom of wildlife." However, long-existing environmental issues, such as air and water pollution, weather changes, soil erosion, desertification, shrinking of natural forests, grassland degradation, and wetland shrinking have upset the home of wild animals and plants and reduced the number of wildlife varieties in the country. As China's huge population is scattered in every corner of the land, the competition for living space between human beings and wildlife are fairly intensive. People in some areas lack the awareness of environmental protection and are eager for quick profits. Consequently they kill wild animals in large numbers and make random use of wild plants, which directly results in the reduction of the varieties of wildlife. Besides, ocean pollution is one of the major causes in doing damage to the variety of living things.

The Chinese government pays great attention to the protection of the variety of wildlife, and has, in recent years, done much work in law making, scientific research, publicity, and building up nature reserves. In order to protect rare animals and plants, the government has promulgated and amended a series of laws and regulations, effectively stopping the damage to wild animal and plant resources. The country now has 1,227 nature reserves, out of which 135 are rated as national-class reserves, covering a total area of 980,000 square kilometers. There are 992 breeding farms for rare animals on the brink of extinction and 50 nurseries for rare plants. Gratifying achievements have been obtained in protecting and breeding rare species on the brink of extinction, such as pandas, golden monkeys, Chinese alligators, south China tigers, and fir trees.

The protection of the varieties of wildlife depends on the concerted efforts of the whole society. To understand that to protect the species' resources is to protect mankind itself, and to develop a civilized ecological consciousness of loving nature and wildlife help mankind to live in harmony with other living things and will prevent the self-destruction of humankind.

8. What Are the Treasures?

China's total verified mineral resources make up about 12 percent of that of the world's total, only next in size to those of the United States and Russia. In per capita resources, however, the Chinese level is quite low, only 58 percent of the world's average. The per capita possession of several major natural resources in the country is one-third or one half of the world's average level. China's iron ore is low in quality, oil reserves are small, and strategic resources are limited. China is, however, rich in coal, tungsten, rare earth, and mineral resources for building materials. China has verified reserves of 155 types of mineral resources, out of which 54 are metallic minerals, 90 are non-metallic minerals, 8 are energy minerals, and 3 are water-gas minerals.

In metallic minerals, China has larger reserves in iron and manganese, compared with that of other countries in the world, but the quality is low. China's verified reserves of iron ore, mainly located in central and west Liaoning Province, central and west Inner Mongolia, Sichuan, and the middle and lower reaches of the Yangtze River, amounts to 45.9 billion tons, but 90 percent of this is of low quality. According to the present mining speed, iron ore reserves can last for about 150 years. The verified reserves of manganese ore are 540 million tons, mostly in poor mines.

China has rich resources of a complete range of non-ferrous minerals. The reserves of bauxite are 2.27 billion tons; copper, 63.07 million tons; lead, 35.10 million tons; and zinc, 92.44 million tons. China leads other countries in its reserves of rare earths and lithium, but has very limited resources of cobalt, gold, and silver, with 41.57 million tons of gold reserves. The copper reserves are mainly located in the middle and lower reaches of the Yangtze River. The resources of tungsten, tin, and antimony are mainly spread out among Hunan, Jiangxi, Guangxi, and Yunnan.

China leads other countries in its reserves of sodium salt and mirabilite for chemical raw materials. The country is rich in low-quality sulfur and phosphorous reserves, specifically 4.4 billion tons of sulfur and iron ore and 13.3 billion tons of phosphorous ore, which are mainly found in southwest and central-south China. The country is short in terms of leopoldite with only a verified reserve of 200 million tons, mainly located in the Qarhan Salt Lake in Qinghai. Compared with the domestic demand for potash fertilizer of 10 million tons in 2000, the reserve is very small. China's verified reserves of boron and natural alkaline are also limited. China is rich in metallurgical supplementary materials, such as magnesite and fluorite, which are traditional export minerals. Flux calcareous rock and dolomite are widely scattered and good in quality. There is a large verified reserve of refractory clay and silica. High temperature refractory materials such as blue talc, andalusite, and sillimanite have a long prospect of tapping. China is also rich in talc, graphite, bentonite, and raw materials for cement, marble, zeolite, perlite, asbestos, and mica. Therefore, China is well poised for developing the building materials industry. China is short in diamonds and the reserves of precious stones are yet to be explored. The reserve of uranium minerals is expected to be around 5,000 tons.

More than half of the 155 minerals that China has developed and used are associated minerals, out of which one-third is under comprehensive development. Every year the country recycles 2.5 million tons of sulfur concentrates and

3.5 million tons of flue sulfuric acid. Each year, China also recycles 42 million tons of steel scraps, which amounts to 41.5 percent of the total annual steel production and is equivalent to saving 168 million tons of iron ore. The yield of non-ferrous metal scraps amounts to about 800,000 tons. The recycled copper makes up 38 percent, lead 20 percent, aluminum 7 percent, and zinc 6 percent of their respective annual output. At present, China needs to import part of its need for iron ore, high quality iron ore, steel products, and copper. From a long-term point of view, China will make up the shortage of iron ore and other minerals by recycling on one hand and importing on the other. The concept of international trading of mineral resources is certainly necessary, but it is equally important to adopt the concept of being self-reliant.

9. In Search of New Energy

In terms of all types of energy, China is rich in coal with a total reserve of about five trillion tons and the verified reserves are another one trillion tons. While China enjoys a rather complete range of different kinds of coals in its reserves, the country is richest in coking coal. Its coal reserves for open-air exploitation amount to 100 billion tons. During the last several years, China has mined 1.3 billion tons of coal each year. Ready reserves of oil and natural gas in the country are not large with a verified reserve of 2.4 billion tons for oil and 961.9 billion cubic meters for natural gas. The future prospect, however, is very promising. The oil reserve in Taklimakan in Xinjiang Uygur Autonomous Region is fairly impressive. According to estimates made by the departments concerned, China's total reserves of oil and gas are 40-60 billion tons.

Hydropower and geothermal energy resources are mainly located in the southwest of China. The steep terrain in western China is home to the sources of several large rivers. Therefore, it is also rich in hydropower resources, with a total water energy reserve of 676 million kilowatts, out of which 56 percent can be developed with an annual power generating capacity of 2,000 billion kilowatts, equivalent to the total amount of electricity generated by all the coal produced in one year in China. With the completion of several hydropower projects, such as the Three Gorges Project, the proportion of hydropower will increase from 8 percent at present to over 30 percent.

Presently, many environmental issues are related to the energy structure. China's coal consumption is over two-thirds of its total energy consumption. The technique for coal application is backward. Desulfurizing, dedusting, gasifying, and liquefying need to be improved without delay. The greenhouse effect, acid rain, and abnormal weather all have something to do with the applications of energy. In environmental protection, there are two ways to better use energy. One is to improve the technology in using energy and the other is to find new energy resources that are clean, efficient, and rich but inexpensive.

To use clean energy sources extensively is a long-time dream of humankind. With the development of science and technology, that day for accomplishing this is not very remote. The latest research results and progress in the development technology of solar, wind, tidal energy, and nuclear fusion have brought new hope to mankind to completely solve energy problems. Solar energy and nuclear fusion, in particular, will be the best solutions to the energy issue. The application of solar energy is a process of transforming the energy with photoelectricity, luminous energy, and actinology into storable energy. Being available at any time and free from pollution, solar energy is an ideal resource. Its extensive use, however, depends on storage costs and efficiency. Consequently there are still some limitations in using solar energy on any big scale. Relatively speaking, nuclear fusion has many advantages while its disadvantages are few. Nuclear fusion is a form of enormous energy released by the atomic nuclei of hydrogen atoms during polymerizing reactions. Its raw material is the isotopes of hydrogen obtainable from seawater. The isotopes of hydrogen obtained from one liter of seawater produce an amount of energy during nuclear fusion equivalent to 300 liters of petroleum. It is really inexhaustible in supply. The elements from nuclear fusion are free from pollution and radiation and therefore it is a clean form of energy. However, nuclear fusion only takes place at high temperature, which makes it difficult for traditional containers to work. This poses the biggest obstacle to the application of nuclear fusion. Researches have been successful in using ceramic containers for nuclear fusion. Thus the application of nuclear fusion in large quantities is not far away.

10. Toward the Blue Ocean

Compared to the oceans, the land on the earth is less than half in size. Therefore the oceans will provide humankind with greater space and richer resources for future development.

The ocean industry will prove an important new industry for mankind in the 21st century. Oceans have inexhaustible resources of water, biology, minerals, and energy. At present, the freshwater on land is in such short supply that some coastal cities are already suffering in their economic development. Desalination is already high on the agenda. The relatively mature technology used in developed countries is ultrafiltration, that is, a separation technology of membrane permeability. Pure water is separated by a semipermeable membrane and pressure technology from other elements in the seawater. A number of coastal cities in China have already used the technology of desalination for commercial drinking water.

China has a coastline of 18,000 kilometers along the continent and 4.73 million square kilometers of ocean with rich resources.

China also has more than 10,000 types of oceanic biological resources such as ocean fish, shrimp, shell fish, crabs, and algae. More than one hundred of these including belt fish, big and small yellow croakers, carpenter's ink markers, sharks, and sea eels produce great yields and are of relatively high economic value. The per capita fishing grounds in China's seas are nearly 2 *mu* (1/15 hectare), equivalent to the per capita farming land space. In 2000, China's fishing production is over 10 million tons, making up one-tenth of the annual world's ocean aquatic production. China's total aquatic production is 25.4 million tons, including more than 10 million tons of shell fish and 3 million tons of shrimp and crabs, which is 1.5 times of the total output of freshwater products. China is the biggest ocean aquatic producer in the world. Among the ocean aquatic products, the quantity of cultivated products occupies nearly half of the total. Therefore, sea aquaculture will provide humankind with new sources of food.

China is also rich in ocean mineral resources such as strategic reserves of petroleum and natural gas. China has a petroleum reserve of 4 to 18 billion tons in the sea and also a considerable reserve of natural gas that is yet to be explored. The ocean manganese nodules are in mineral beds of nonferrous metals, nodules containing mainly manganese and nickel, copper, etc. They will prove to be important future metal resources. Seawater also contains many vital chemical components, known as "liquid minerals," such as chlorine, sodium, calcium, potassium, and magnesium. These will provide mankind with an almost endless supply of mineral reserves.

The oceans also have power sources such as power generated by tides, waves, and currents in the coastal areas. According to estimates, China has a theoretical tidal power reserve of 110 million kilowatts and a wave power reserve of 150 million kilowatts. The potential for developing energy with temperature difference is even greater. Such technology is now being studied and developed. In space resources and tourism resources, the oceans also boast great potential. Cities on the sea and sea tourism will be new fashions for living and recreation in the 21st century.

At present, however, the oceans are being severely polluted and damaged with the frequent occurrence of red tides. Owing to excessive fishing, the coastal fish species have drastically declined. It is of prime importance to control pollutant emissions into the seas, through administrative, legal, and economic measures in order to protect the ocean's biological elements and ensure the hygienic security of aquatic products. At present, the departments concerned have already introduced laws and regulations to protect the seas so that the ocean's biological resources can be utilized in a sustainable way.

Environmental issues are the result of conflicts between the social development of mankind and nature. Therefore, the problems have to be solved by mankind itself. With the progress of technology and management and with high attention paid by the whole of mankind to environmental protection, man will be able to enjoy a beautiful future.

(Written by Liu Zhiyan)

Chapter 9 The Reunification of the Country and Unity of the Nation

In the development of mankind, the Chinese civilization is famous for its ancient, uninterrupted and profound history. Today, along with the implementation of the reform and opening up program and the constant progress in the modernization drive, the Chinese people's wishes for the reunification of the country are being realized one after another. And the rallying power of the Chinese nation has become further strengthened. The return of Hong Kong and Macao has aroused the pride of the Chinese people. Every year more and more Taiwan compatriots come to the mainland to visit relatives and friends, make investments, study, and do sightseeing. Increasing contacts between the Chinese on both sides of the Taiwan Straits indicate that the trend of reunification of the whole country is a common wish of the people both in Taiwan and the mainland.

Many countries and regions have ethnic disputes and even violent conflicts. The 56 ethnic groups in China are united closely on an equal footing for mutual benefit and joint prosperity. China is a country in which there are autonomous regions for areas inhabited by ethnic minorities so as to promote the development of the ethnic minority regions on the largest scale. People of all the ethnic groups in China work closely hand in hand and shoulder to shoulder for common development. The achievements and experience in the unity and progress of the nation are worthy of pride.

1. "One China": an Inevitable Trend

From ancient times, Taiwan has been part of China and has always maintained the traditional Chinese culture. These are indisputable facts. The 26th Conference of the United Nations in 1971 passed the Resolution No. 2758 to expel the "representatives" of the Kuomintang (Nationalist) Party from Taiwan, and to restore the seat and all the legal rights in the United Nations to the People's Republic of China. Up to now, over 160 countries have established diplomatic relations with China. They all admit that there is only one China and Taiwan is a part of China, and that the government of the People's Republic of China is the only legal representative of the country.

Taiwan belongs to all the Chinese people. Actually the majority of people on Taiwan Island long for peace, stability, and development. Only about 5 percent of the people in Taiwan support "Taiwan independence," while more than 80 percent stand for the status quo or reunification with the motherland. One investigation made by ETTV in Taiwan showed that after Chen Shui-bian made his statement of "one country on each side of the Taiwan Straits," his support dropped to a new record low of only 46 percent. Another investigation result revealed by the *China Times*, a newspaper with a large circulation, showed that 49 percent of the interviewees expressed dissatisfaction with Chen' statement for the way to deal with relations between Taiwan and the mainland. The latest investigation has shown that 51 percent of the people in Taiwan support the principle of "one country, two systems." The opposition alliance, consisting of the Kuomintang, People First Party, and the New Party, are strongly opposed to Chen Shui-bian's statement for "Taiwan independence" and they have requested that the Taiwan authorities return to the "common understanding of 1992." The business circles in Taiwan have made strong requests in a number of ways, such as a statement with 10,000 characters, asking the Taiwan authorities to return to the "common understanding of 1992," to start political negotiations between both sides of the Taiwan Straits, to stop the stance of "no urgency, more patience," and to open three direct links of trade, mail, and air and shipping services across the Taiwan Straits so as to pull the island out of its economic recession.

During the last several years, the aggregate economic strength of the mainland has continually expanded and the mainland occupies an obvious leading position in the relations between both sides of the Taiwan Straits. On October 9, 2001, General Secretary of the CPC and President of China Jiang Zemin stressed in his speech marking the 90th anniversary of the Revolution of 1911 that "Taiwan should neither avoid nor be obscure" on the one-China principle. After Chen Shui-bian made the statement of "one country on each side of the Straits," the Chinese government strongly condemned it, warning separatists in Taiwan to pull back before it was too late, and to stop any separatist activities. Besides this, the framework of "one China" is stronger in the international community. The Taiwan authorities' attempts to join the United Nations and the World Heath Organization, and to create "two Chinas" and "one China, one Taiwan" have been met with failure.

2. Reunification of the Motherland: a Relentless Pursuit

"Reunification will be beneficial to either side while separation harms both sides." As early as in the 1950s, the Chinese government tried to solve the Taiwan issue in a peaceful way. Mao Zedong made proposals about "peace, the best option," "all patriots coming together as one family," and "being patriotic without distinction of time sequence."

Since the 3rd Plenary of the 11th Central Committee of the CPC, the Chinese Communist Party and the government have put forward the policies of "peaceful reunification" and "one country, two systems." Since January 1, 1979, the Chinese People's Liberation Army has stopped the bombing of the Greater Jinmen, Lesser Jinmen, Dadan, and Erdan islands, which are under the control of the Taiwan authorities. On the same day, the Standing Committee of the National People's Congress issued a "Message to Taiwan Compatriots." These steps marked an important adjustment in the Party and government's guiding policy, from one of "liberating Taiwan" to one of "peaceful reunification."

In September, 1981, Ye Jianying, then chairman of the Standing Committee of the NPC, made a speech elaborating in an all-round way the guiding policies about the return of Taiwan to the mainland and the realization of peaceful reunification, known ever since as the "Ye's Nine Principles." This marked a further step in the development of the Party's policies toward Taiwan in the new historic period, and it is also a major symbol of the mature concept of "one country, two systems." In a speech by Deng Xiaoping in January 1982, he said that "The nine principles made in the name of

Ye Jianying actually mean the policy of "one country, two systems." This was the first time that Deng Xiaoping put forward the concept of "one country, two systems" in his position as the leader of the Party. On June 25, 1983, he reiterated six points with regard to how to solve the Taiwan issue through the policy of "one country, two systems" and to realize the reunification of the country. This speech was called "Deng's Six Principles," and it was a complete, clear, and systematic statement of the concept of "one country, two systems."

On October 12, 1992, General Secretary Jiang Zemin stated in his report to the 14th National Congress of the CPC that the Kuomintang and the Communist Party should start negotiations on formally ending the state of hostility between both sides of the Taiwan Straits and gradually realize a peaceful reunification. With the active promotion of the correct guiding policies made by the third generation of the collective leadership of the CPC, with Jiang Zemin at the core, the relations between both sides of the Taiwan Straits during the several years of the 1990s and especially after 1992 have developed remarkably.

In September 1993, the Taiwan Affairs Office and Information Office of the State Council jointly issued a white paper on *The Issue of Taiwan and China's Reunification*. This was the first governmental document systematically outlining the question of Taiwan and the Chinese government's basic policies to settle the Taiwan issue. Jiang Zemin made an important speech on January 30, 1995, with the title "To Strive Continuously for the Reunification of the Motherland," that fully stated the Chinese government's policies on the way to settle the Taiwan question and to realize the reunification of the country. He raised eight points about the present development of relations between both sides of the Taiwan Straits and the promotion of the peaceful reunification of the country. These eight positions later became known as "Jiang's Eight Positions," and they have played a guiding role and exerted profound influence on the development of relations between both sides of the Taiwan Straits and the problem of peaceful reunification, a fact that has been approved by the development in recent years and will be further reflected in the years ahead.

In January 2002, Qian Qichen, vice premier and member of the Politburo of the Central Committee of the CPC, made an important speech at the 7th anniversary of the release of "Jiang's Eight Positions," which he said had shown the strongest sincerity and greatest magnanimity on the part of the mainland in breaking the deadlock between both sides of the Taiwan Straits and promoting dialogues and negotiations between the two sides. As long as the Taiwan side takes serious and active steps on the basis of the "common understanding of 1992," the two sides can make steps forward and bring the relations to a new stage.

3. How Far Away Are the "Three Direct Links"?

In the spring of 1979 and of 1980, the Standing Committee of the National People's Congress and the Chinese People's Political Consultative Conference issued a "Message to Taiwan Compatriots" and a Spring Festival Greeting letter calling for three direct links in trade, mail, air and shipping services across the Taiwan Straits. With a strong promotion of "three links," the relations between both sides of the Taiwan Straits have changed greatly since the 1980s from that of separations to contacts and from that of hostility to moderation.

Since July 28, 1987, the Taiwan authorities have lifted their ban on going sightseeing in Hong Kong and Macao, allowing Taiwan citizens to go to the mainland via Hong Kong or Macao. Later the authorities agreed to allow Taiwan citizens, except for military men in active service and public servants, to go to the mainland to visit relatives with bonds of blood or marriage.

To meet the demand for the exchanges of people on both sides of the Taiwan Straits, the Taiwan Straits Exchange Foundation and Association for Relations Across the Taiwan Straits were set up in the early 1990s. In 1992, the two organizations reached an oral consensus that "both sides of the Straits should persist in the principle of one China." In April 1993, the two organizations held a meeting in Singapore headed by Wang and Koo from both sides, reaching an agreement concerning exchanges and visits in the fields of economy, science and technology, culture, and education. The two sides also agreed on establishment of contacts and talks between the two organizations. The "Wang-Koo Talks" were discussions by the two sides at the highest level, conducted in an unofficial manner after 1949, symbolizing a historically important step in the relations between the people on both sides of the Taiwan Straits.

In recent years, there have been more and more unofficial contacts between both sides. Taiwan investors have made vigorous investments in Shanghai, Qingdao, and the western region of China. And between January and October of 2001, the mainland approved 3,312 new Taiwanese investment projects, 36.97 percent higher than had been approved in the same period of 2000, with US $5.322 billion in investments contracted from Taiwan, 71.34 percent higher than that during the same period the year before. The actual utilization of Taiwan capital was US $2.398 billion, 37.37 percent higher than for the same period of 2000.

During the first half of 2002, Taiwan's exports to the United States, Europe, and Japan continued to decrease, but those to Asia increased by 6.3 percent. Exports to Hong Kong, South Korea, and China's mainland increased considerably. Hong Kong has become the largest importer of Taiwan's exports and the mainland has become the place with the highest growth rate of Taiwan's exports. Taiwan's exports to Hong Kong and the mainland reached US $187.1 billion, including transit exports from Hong Kong to the mainland. Taiwan's exports to the mainland went from 3.53 percent of its total export volume in 2001 to 6.22 percent in the first half of 2002, indicating the close trade contacts that now exist between both sides of the Taiwan Straits.

During the first ten months of 2001, the number of Taiwan compatriots coming to the mainland to visit relatives, sightsee, study, do business, and engage in commercial exchanges was over two million. The year of 2001 was a record year for cultural exchanges between both sides, totaling 350 projects. In all, 140 universities and colleges on the mainland accepted 4,000 Taiwan students. In 2001, the number of Taiwan students applying for study at Peking University was three times of that in 2000. Many leading senior middle school graduates gave up the opportunity to study at universities in Taiwan, instead choosing to study at universities on the mainland.

With both sides' accession to the WTO, Taiwan citizens, especially those from industrial and commercial circles, strongly requested that the Taiwan authorities relax their restrictions and realize the "three direct links" as early as possible. Mass media in Taiwan have revealed that the latest poll among the people showed that 70 percent of them have asked for early "three direct links" so that Taiwan can have more room for development. Recently delegations advocating the "three direct links," consisting of the personnel from the political, industrial, and business circles in Taiwan, have frequently visited the mainland. This reflects the Taiwan compatriots' urgent demand for "three direct links," and the interests of the majority of people in Taiwan.

4. Pearl in the East: Prosperous as Before

Since the return of Hong Kong to the mainland, the policy of "one country, two systems" has undergone different tests and has proved to be successful. Hong Kong continues to maintain its original characteristics and advantages, attracting investors from different countries and playing a key role in the new pattern of China's opening to the outside world.

Since its return, Hong Kong as an economic entity continues to maintain its powerful competitiveness in the world. It is the most important international financial and transit center, with the biggest port for loading and unloading containers, largest international airport, largest and most advanced airport for cargo, second largest management center for vessels, fourth largest gold market, fifth biggest foreign exchange market, tenth largest stock market (the third largest in Asia), the economic zone with the greatest freedom, and the sixth most competitive region in the world.

Not long ago, Hong Kong won 8.8 points more than Singapore and the United States as the economic zone with the greatest degree of trade freedom. According to statistics published by the Hong Kong government, up to June 2001, there were 3,237 regional headquarters and offices of foreign companies stationed in Hong Kong, which marked a new record high.

Since its return to the motherland, Hong Kong has had closer economic ties with the mainland, its intermediary position has been strengthened, and the mainland has become the important backup for economic development and prosperity in Hong Kong. According to the statistics of the Hong Kong Customs, the trade volume between the mainland and Hong Kong went up from US $78 billion in 1997 to US $157.5 billion in 2001. Hong Kong is the largest transit place for the mainland, the third largest trading partner, and the second largest export market for the mainland. The mainland has also become Hong Kong's largest destination for its export products (in 2001, overtaking the United States for the first time), import products, and transit trade.

Since 1997, Hong Kong has continuously increased its investments in the mainland. Presently Hong Kong's investment projects on the mainland are over 180,000 with a contracted amount over US $350 billion and actual investment over US $180 billion. For Hong Kong, the mainland is the largest investment area outside the territory of Hong Kong. Meanwhile a great deal of inland capital has also flown to Hong Kong. According to an incomplete calculation, every year about US $1 to 2 billion flows from the mainland into the Hong Kong stock market. The Hong Kong economic yearbook suggested that up to the end of 1999, the mainland had made direct investments in Hong Kong totaling HK $814.8 billion (US $104.5 billion). Now more than 2,000 enterprises from the mainland have been involved in finance, trading, service, etc. in Hong Kong. Since the 1990s, H shares and red chip shares based on companies from the mainland and listed in the Hong Kong stock market have raised more than HK $243.1 billion for the H shares, and raised HK $103.3 billion for the red chip shares. At present, these two types of shares take up 40 percent of the total value of the Hong Kong stock market.

The mainland is the largest place of origin for tourists to Hong Kong, which has become a major destination for mainland tourists. The number of tourists from the mainland to Hong Kong increased from 2.3 million in 1997 to 4.45 million in 2001, bringing enormous economic benefits to Hong Kong, specifically amounting to HK $23 billion in 2001. Hong Kong compatriots are also the largest source of tourists and commercial customers for the mainland. In 2000, the number of Hong Kong visitors to the mainland for the first time reached 50 million, and in 2001, 52 million.

5. "One Country, Two Systems" Showing Vitality in Macao

On December 20, 1999, Macao returned to the motherland. The Hong Kong newspaper *The Oriental* said in an editorial that "From this day on there will be no foreign control on every inch of the land of China."

Since the return of Macao, the policy of "one country, two systems, and the governing of Macao by its own people" has been successfully practiced. The government in the

Macao Special Administrative Region headed by Edmund Ho Hau Wah, the chief executive, has been leading Macao residents in making joint efforts, in accordance with the policy of "consolidating the economic base and developing with stability," changing the situation of minus economic growth for several consecutive years and the social chaos that occurred before its return to the motherland.

Since the return, the government of the Macao SAR has put forward social security as its first priority, and has taken a series of measures to crack down on criminal activities. The second year after its return saw a marginal decrease in the crime rate in Macao. During the first half of 2001, the number of serious cases of crime went down by 37 percent. During the first half of 2002, the number of vicious cases was reduced again, and juvenile criminal cases declined by 32.2 percent. The mass media in Macao has commented on the fact that up to now one of the biggest advantages of Macao's return to the motherland is that the citizens have a more secure living environment.

Before its return to the motherland, Macao suffered from four consecutive years of minus economic growth. In the first year after its return, however, the economy grew by 4 percent in Macao. Zhu Rongji, China's premier at that time, praised this saying it was a remarkable achievement.

From 2002, Macao has entered a new round of economic growth. During the first half of 2002, Macao received 5.48 million tourists, 9.3 percent higher than that for the same period of 2001. Since the opening up of its lottery business, its income has increased. An income tax of 3.45 billion Macao dollars from lottery was paid to the government during the first half of 2002, 9 percent higher than for the same period of 2001. During the first five months in 2002, the total export value in Macao was 6.7 billion Macao dollars, 0.4 percent higher than that for the same period of 2001. And between March and May in 2002, the unemployment rate was 6.2 percent, slightly lower in comparison with the same period of 2001. According to calculation of the departments concerned, economic growth in Macao in 2002 was 5 percent, a record year since 1994.

The basic rights of Macao's citizens since its return to China have been guaranteed to a maximum extent and they continue to enjoy freedom of speech, press, and association according to law. Macao's multi-cultural features have been respected. With an attitude of being the masters of Macao, the residents have participated in all the affairs in the Macao SAR. The second legislative conference was held in the Macao SAR in September 2002, being the first to which elected representatives were seated after the establishment of the Macao SAR. As many as 160,000 people turned out for the election. It was a record year with the largest number of voters. There were 15 electoral colleges, which also marked a new record.

6. Development of the West: Pushing Forward National Development

The Chinese government's proposal of a strategy for developing the western regions, first publicized in June 1999, was officially launched in January 2001. Out of the total of 55 ethnic minority groups in the country, 48 live in the west and most of the country's autonomous regions, which occupy 86 percent of the land area in the west, are also located in this region. For the strategy of developing the west, the government has emphasized "The purpose of carrying out the strategy is to speed up the development among minority ethnic groups and the areas in which they reside."

Since the implementation of the strategy, there has been a great surge from the making of strategic plans and policies to the implementation of key projects, from publicity campaigns and mobilization drives to attracting investments in the west. So far, the growth rate in investments in the west has exceeded that in the east and central China. In Inner Mongolia alone, the Central Government has invested more than 3 billion yuan during the last two years for the purpose of converting former farmlands to forestry and pastureland, controlling the shifting sands, protecting natural forests, and the conservation of soil and water.

By the end of 2001, economic growth in the ethnic minority autonomous regions of Inner Mongolia, Guangxi, Tibet, Ningxia, Xinjiang, and ethnic areas in the provinces of Yunnan, Guizhou, and Qinghai has been higher than the average national growth rate for five consecutive years. In the first three quarters of 2002, the GDP growth in Qinghai and Ningxia was 12.4 and 10.3 percent respectively, higher than that in many provinces in the east and central China. Specifically the margins of their GDP increase are respectively the highest and the fifth highest in the whole country.

During the first three quarters of 2002, investment in fixed assets in the west increased by 24.5 percent, 5.4 percent higher than the same period of 2001, 7.2 and 3.4 percent higher than that for east and central China. Investment increased most quickly in Guizhou (54.9 percent), Qinghai (32.9 percent), Ningxia (34.4 percent) and Xinjiang (29.5 percent). To assist in implementing the strategy of developing the west, the Central Government allocated 30 billion yuan from the 150 billion yuan raised through the national construction bonds in 2002. More funding from the Central Government and the increase of local funds and capital from east China have given impetus to the investment in fixed assets in the west in 2002.

The construction speed of large- and medium-sized projects in the west has been fast as well. In 2000, 40 percent of the on-going projects were either completed or partly completed for production. The construction of new projects has been going smoothly. The ecological projects, such as those for converting farmland to forests, protecting natural forests, sand control around Beijing and Tianjin, and restoring natural grasslands have been going well too. Faster steps have been taken in training more talented persons and enhancing science, education, and social development. In 2000, the investment in fixed assets in 12 provinces and autonomous regions in the west increased by about 15 percent in comparison with 1999, higher than the average rate of 9.3 percent in the whole country; and the GDP growth was 8.5 percent, also higher than 1999.

The development in the west has had an all around impact on the areas in which the minority ethnic groups reside. People's concepts, for example, have gradually changed; local governments have developed a better consciousness of service; enterprises have taken a greater degree of awareness in competition, and the people are much clearer about the market economy.

It should be noted, however, that there are still big gaps between the economic development in the west and other areas of the country. Owing to historical and geographical factors in all the provinces and autonomous regions in the west, there are a large proportion of state-owned enterprises, especially military enterprises, while the development of privately-run enterprises is far behind that in the eastern part of the country. In the list of "100 top private enterprises," only 13 are from the 12 western provinces and autonomous regions, fewer than those in the eastern Zhejiang Province alone. This falling behind of the private economy has caused a widening of the gaps between different areas and has led to the backwardness of the west.

The west is still in the preliminary stage of development. Preparations should be made to tackle correctly the relations among infrastructure projects, eco-environment, restructuring of the economy, and science and education so as to correctly deal with the relationship among support from the Central Government, from the developed areas, and the local efforts from the ethnic minority regions. This will enable the right handling of the relationship among all ethnic groups in the west, and the "building of a beautiful land" will not just be a slogan, but will be turned into reality. In this way people in the west will no longer carry the burden of a minus growth rate in the economy.

7. Autonomy in Ethnic Minority Regions: Catching the Attention of the World

Since the 1950s, China has wiped out ethnic depression and discrimination, carried out the policy that all ethnic groups in the country are equal, created a system of regional autonomy in ethnic minority regions, and gradually established new relationships among different ethnic groups on the basis of equality, unity, friendship, and mutual help. These developments have played a key role in the political, economic, and cultural development of the ethnic minority regions.

General Secretary Jiang Zemin greatly appreciated this during his inspection tour of Xinjiang in July 1998. He pointed out that "In looking back at China's history of several thousand years, ethnic policies in the New China are the best. In comparison with other countries, our ethnic policies have proved to be most successful". Especially the system of autonomy in the minority ethnic regions is a model for dealing with relations among different ethnic groups in a unified country. In February 2001, in summing up the successful experiences of this system, the Standing Committee of the National People's Congress made amendments to the law of autonomy in minority ethnic regions which confirmed that "This system is one of the basic political systems in the country."

China is the only country in the world carrying out a system of minority regional autonomy, whose main feature is the organic combination of unification with autonomy. Up to now, a total of 155 places consisting of 120 autonomous counties, 30 autonomous prefectures, and 5 autonomous regions have been set up in the country.

Areas resided in by ethnic minorities in China before 1949 used to have different political systems such as the banner and league systems, the system of temporal and religious administrations, the rule of a local headman, mountain official, and the rule of a senior person as in the case of the Yao people. These systems could not operate under the central government's policies and decrees, could not help maintain the country's unified sovereignty, and could be easily be used by aggressive foreign forces. The promotion of ethnic minority regional autonomy has completely changed the status of separation in many ethnic regions in the past. The performance of regional autonomy has effectively guaranteed the equal democratic rights of ethnic minority groups, their rights to manage their own ethnic affairs, and to actively promote local economic construction and social development in the ethnic regional autonomous areas.

The ethnic minorities who live scattered rather than their own compact communities have also obtained full attention. Autonomous towns as a supplementary model of ethnic regional autonomy have also developed greatly. By the end of 2000, China had 1,213 autonomous townships (towns). Except for Shanghai, Ningxia, and Shanxi, all other provinces and autonomous regions have ethnic autonomous townships (towns) with a combined population of 9.48 million persons, which is about one-third of the population of all the ethnic minority groups who live scattered in different parts of the country. As a result of historical and natural factors, most of the ethnic townships (towns) are located in remote border regions and mountainous areas where the living standards are low, the economy is poor, and the cultural development is backward. The central and local governments at all levels have introduced policies and regulations to help develop in an all around way the economies and cultures in the ethnic townships (towns).

"The Implementation Rules for Ethnic Townships (Towns)" issued by the State Council in 1993 was a legal document for the people of minority ethnic groups who live in different parts of China and who, until then, had no laws for their own protection. There have been all types of support and co-operation from municipal and provincial governmental organizations to the ethnic townships (towns) and between the better-off and poor ethnic townships (towns).

In recent years, the ethnic townships (towns) have experienced faster economic development and higher living standards. According to the statistics of the State Ethnic Affairs Commission, between 1996 and 2000, the total agricultural production value and industrial production value in all the ethnic townships (towns) increased by 8 and 11.3 percent annually on average, hitting the figures of 41.5 and 59.5 billion yuan respectively at the end of 2000, with a net per capita income of 1,674 yuan, thus changing them from poverty to a life of adequate food and clothing.

8. Multicultural Protection, Development and Application

Culture is the root of a nation, a precious form of spiritual wealth and human resources accumulated by a nation over a long time. The Chinese nation is a joint entity with multi-ethnic groups. A fundamental way to help ethnic minority groups to get involved in development together is to fully recognize and take into consideration the special human condition of multiple cultures in west China. In recent years, China's stress of giving attention, protection, and development to the multi-cultures of ethnic minority groups is virtually giving attention to the relationship between the trend of modernization and the reality of traditional culture.

Upsurges of returning to traditional cultures have occurred in the midst of the development of a modern social and market economic system since the 1990s. In large cities, "ethnic villages" and "ethnic parks" have been built. Construction of ethnic villages has become a new hotspot for business investments in Shenzhen, Beijing, Kunming, Dalian, Qingdao, Changsha, etc. Ethnic villages constructed to their original size or in miniature, with copies of the natural scenery, views, and ethnic features, have appeared one after another both in the north and south of China.

In 1997, the construction of the first ecological museum in China began in Suoga, a Miao, Yi and Hui ethnic township, along the Sancha River near Liuzhi in southwestern Guizhou Province. This museum is a science study project in co-operation between museum circles in China and Norway. This project is based on a Miao community in Suoga, where the horn of a bull is used as a head decoration. The purpose is to combine the theory of an ecological museum with the specific situation in China, building an ecological museum with "a world language" that can be acknowledged by the international community and can protect the natural and cultural environments in that community as well as promote its social, economic, and cultural progress.

The culture of the ethnic minority groups has been vigorously developed from being dull and monotonous to being colorful, and from being passively accepted to one of active participation. The Nadam sports meets of the Mongolians; singing accompanied by traditional instruments of the Uygur, Kazakh, and Kirghiz people; the singing contests of the Hui people; and the festival marking the anniversary of westward migration of the Xibe people have become regular activities in places where these ethnic minorities reside. And each time such activities are held, there are new creative forms to the delight of the local residents. As a result, these have become major forms of mass cultural activities in rural areas and the pastureland. People from different ethnic groups are fond of their cultural life and they are not satisfied with being only spectators. Instead, they want to participate, to be creative, and to be the actual performers.

Many local governments encourage and financially support these ethnic and folk activities so that they can display the distinctive features and attractions of the cultures of different ethnic groups in their own areas. For example, the government of Ningxia Hui Autonomous Region mobilizes social communities to run competitions of Hui people's singing contests that are held in scenic spots, cultural performances in the spring, and cultural competitions in the whole autonomous region during the Spring Festival.

9. "Three Non-separations": Increasingly Popular

Ethnic contradictions and conflicts have become intensified worldwide since the 1990s. National separatism has resulted in disintegration of several countries. Racial violence and religious nationalism have been exceptionally active so that in some countries and regions local nationalism and tribalism have stirred up continued instabilities and led to bloodshed.

Relatively speaking, the relationships among all ethnic groups in China are harmonious, equal, united, and mutually helpful though China still has some ethnic problems. China's experiences in dealing with ethnic issues have been successful and widely recognized. Opening up the world map, it is only too easy to find that the Fergana Basin in the heart of the Eurasian continent has become a base camp for terrorism. Poor and backward, this region has complicated ethnic and religious contradictions with three kinds of sinister forces: separatists, religious extremists, and terrorists. These three forces engage in frantic actions in Central Asia, turning the region into a center and base camp for international terrorists. Central Asia borders China's northwest. Extremist religious forces and national separatist forces not only take Central Asia as their base, frequently molding public opinion in an attempt to separate China, but also try to penetrate the national boundaries into northwest China. On June 14, 2001, China, Russia, Kazakhstan, Kirghizstan, Tadzhikistan, and Uzbekistan launched in Shanghai "the Shanghai Organization for Co-operation," a model to attack international terrorists through international co-operation. Recently the United Nations and countries concerned have officially announced that the Eastern Turkistan Islamic Movement (ETIM) is on the list of "international terrorist organizations." This proves that the fight against terrorists and national separatists has become a common understanding in the international community.

In July 1998, on his inspection tour of Xinjiang, General Secretary Jiang Zemin pointed out that a concept that the 56 ethnic groups in China are all equal members of the Chinese big family had to be formed. The Han ethnic group cannot be separated from ethnic minority groups, which in turn cannot be separated from the Han ethnic group, and none of the ethnic minority groups can be separated from one another. Working together shoulder to shoulder and sharing the same destiny, the people of all ethnic groups should strive for the construction of a socialist country with Chinese characteristics. Therefore, the Chinese people must be good at distinguishing and correctly tackling the contradictions between ourselves and our enemies, and the contradictions among the people. Meanwhile, people of all ethnic groups must focus on economic construction. Without economic and cultural development, there will be a series of problems including those caused by ethnic issues.

10. The Merits of Overseas Chinese

An old saying goes that wherever there is seawater, there are Chinese. Chinese have become a major force in promoting the development of civilizations of mankind. At present, besides China's mainland, Taiwan, Hong Kong, and Macao, there are over 30 million Chinese living in 136 countries and regions in the world. They constitute the largest overseas population of a single ethnic origin, which is scattered the most extensively in the world today. From the very beginning, the Chinese tried to make a living with "three cutters", i.e., a hair-cutting tool, a pair of tailor's scissors, and a kitchen knife. From there, they have extended their business to commerce, manufacturing, real estate, tourism, hi-tech, finance, and other service industries.

According to incomplete statistics, at the end of 2000, the annual income of overseas Chinese was about US $300 billion. Together with the overseas Arab and Jewish people, the Chinese represent one of the three strongest financial forces among all foreign nationals of the world, exerting a great influence on the economic development of Asia, the Pacific regions, and other continents in the world. They have spread the Chinese civilization and enriched the culture in all countries and regions where they have settled. As overseas Chinese, they are concerned with the future of their motherland and many of them have returned to make contributions to this country.

In the history of the People's Republic of China, there have been two waves of the return in large numbers of Chinese intellectuals from abroad. The first was between 1949 and 1950 when many overseas Chinese gave up good incomes abroad to return to the motherland to join in the construction of New China. The second wave was between 1997 and the beginning of 2000, when many IT professionals came back to China to set up IT companies or to participate in IT projects invested in by transnational companies. They have shown the world that China is in step with the world in terms of science and technology concepts. Now a third wave will soon begin. Many young people studying abroad will come back to seek business opportunities in China. According to *Lianhe Zaobao*, a Chinese-language newspaper in Singapore, a questionnaire circulated to the overseas Chinese at the end of August 2001 showed that 48.69 percent of the people expressed their willingness to work in China. In recent years, the number of returned overseas students has increased by 13 percent each year. So far over 130,000 have come back to work.

Over the past two decades, China has received more than US $600 billion in foreign capital, of which most was from overseas Chinese businessmen or was introduced with their assistance. The enterprises they run have helped the economy grow in the coastal cities and other areas of China. In other words, the overseas Chinese have shown great merit in the great achievements of the Chinese economy.

The overseas Chinese love China and have been a strong force in the promotion of the reunification of the motherland.

According to an incomplete calculation, there are more than eighty organizations of overseas Chinese that are against Taiwan's independence and for the reunification. This clearly indicates that the overseas Chinese have realized the importance of reuniting the country. They themselves have organized and taken action, forming a key force of opposition to Taiwan independence and for the support of reunification. Conferences on Opposing Taiwan Independence and Supporting Reunification have been held in Berlin, Washington, and other cities during the last several years. By doing so, the overseas Chinese have played an important role in opposing Taiwan independence and enhancing their morale and will for reunification. To a great extent, they have reduced and offset the effect of the "theory of a threat from China," "the theory of containing China," and support for Taiwan independence that have been voiced time and again by international anti-China forces.

(Written by Zhang Guanxin)

Chapter 10 China and the World

When meeting the Brazilian President Joao Baptista de Oliveira Figueiredo on May 29, 1984, Chinese leader Deng Xiaoping for the first time elaborated in a systematic manner the two great trends in the world: peace and development. He explicitly pointed out: "The aim of our foreign policy is world peace. Always bearing that aim in mind, we are wholeheartedly devoting ourselves to the modernization program to develop our country and to build socialism with Chinese characteristics."

In his speech to commemorate the 80th anniversary of the founding of the Communist Party On July 1, 2001, Jiang Zemin, Party General Secretary and President of China, said: "The purposes of China's foreign policy are to safeguard world peace and promote common development. We adhere to an independent foreign policy of peace. We have carried out friendly exchanges and mutually beneficial cooperation with all countries and have treated one another as equals on the basis of the Five Principles of Peaceful Coexistence in a ceaseless effort to advance the cause of human progress."

Chinese leaders are not only advocates but also sincere implementers of peaceful diplomacy. During the last decade and more, China, through peaceful negotiations and friendly consultations, has solved issues with most of its neighboring countries that had been left unsolved by history. In dealing with difficult disputes over territory and sovereignty, the Chinese leaders have creatively put forward a peaceful stance of "shelving disputes and joint development." With far-sighted political courage, the Chinese leaders have put forward the principle of "increasing trust, reducing trouble, cooperation in development, and not engaging in conflicts" in dealing with the Sino-US relations that have experienced constant friction. This move has dissolved many of the conflicts and disputes, which are almost unavoidable in Sino-US relations.

1. Peace: Theme of the Century in Chinese Diplomacy

As many people know, domestic and external environments faced by the second and third generation leaders of the Communist Party were quite different from those before. Internationally, by 2001 the Cold War had become a matter of history and an all-round world war had become something hard to imagine. Domestically, China's reform had achieved gigantic success, the socialist market economic system has been basically established, the national economy continued to increase at a high speed and people's lives had greatly improved. Faced with different domestic and international environments at different times, two generations of CPC leaders, however, have spoken with a common voice, emphasizing their desire to strive for and safeguard world peace. They had spared no effort in making that the major goal of China's diplomacy. This was by no means accidental.

In a general sense, just as the far-sightedness of the two

generations of the central leaders, neither of the two topics of peace and development has so far been settled, and "the world still remains very unstable." Therefore, to maintain world peace and promote international cooperation are the responsibilities and moral position of China as a member of the Security Council of the United Nations. What is more important is that both generations of central leaders have had an insight into history and have profoundly realized the significance of lasting peace to the Chinese nation, which had suffered from wars and internal turmoil for more than a hundred years. Without a peaceful and stable international environment, China cannot achieve fundamental success in its program of reform and opening to the outside world. Without lasting world peace, the great revitalization of the Chinese nation will only be a dream. Last, but not the least, China's socialist system and policies of reform and opening up to the outside world are in opposition to any pursuit for world peace through war. Meanwhile, the price of war is getting higher and higher. There is no victor in a war. Peace is the most effective solution to maintain national interests and realize the national aspirations of a country.

2. Transcending Ideological Gaps

At the turn of the decade from the 1980s to the 1990s, the entire international community underwent the most dramatic political change since World War II. The Yalta mechanism, which had been the pillar of the world for half a century, suddenly collapsed. Under such a severe international situation, China's foreign policy faced two major challenges: the first was how to evaluate and deal with the dramatic changes in Eastern Europe and the former Soviet Union, what principles and measures to take in dealing with the relations between China and those ex-socialist countries, the parties in power and their political leaders; the second was how to break as early as possible the sanctions imposed by the Western countries on China and restore normal economic and trade relations and political contacts with the developed countries. In the face of the dramatic changes in the world, Chinese leader Deng Xiaoping gave three pieces of advice to his comrades in the Party: "Observing the situation calmly, maintaining our positions firmly, and dealing with the challenges confidently." He advised the Party to "be calm, calm, and calm again. Engage ourselves in our own work unostentatiously and be sure to manage our own affairs well."

The third generation of collective leadership, with Jiang Zemin at the core, creatively applied Deng Xiaoping's principles in foreign affairs and soon mapped out strategies to tackle the unfavorable situations. The key points of the strategy were: to continue the policies of reform and opening up to the outside world and to display to the international community the consistency in China's domestic and external policies; not to hinder the development of state relations with other countries by differences in social systems, ideologies, and values; and not to interfere with the internal affairs of other countries, but to respect the choices of the people of other countries.

In order to implement these foreign policy objectives, the Chinese leaders conducted frequent diplomatic activities at the beginning of the 1990s. In 1991, Chinese leaders paid visits to more than thirty countries in Asia, Africa, Latin America, and Europe and received more than a hundred state and government leaders and other senior officials from other countries. In 1992, Chinese leaders visited 48 countries on the five continents and received more than 60 foreign leaders visiting China, including 24 heads of state, 10 heads of government, and 17 foreign ministers. In 1993, Chinese leaders paid visits to 45 countries and received 78 foreign leaders including foreign ministers. At the beginning of the 1990s, China accomplished a series of well-known diplomatic achievements by correctly responding to the challenges and taking high-level and highly frequent diplomatic initiatives.

It is worthwhile to note that in transcending the differences in political systems, ideologies, and values, China has made great success in promoting relations with a number of countries in an all-round way. Along its borders, China established diplomatic relations with Singapore, Brunei, and South Korea, and restored normal relations with Viet Nam. China made great progress in implementing policies of friendship with neighboring countries. In Eastern Europe and the former Soviet Union, China on one hand strengthened friendly diplomatic relations with the countries with which China already had diplomatic ties, and on the other, respected the choices of the people of these countries and quickly recognized the newly independent countries by establishing diplomatic relations with them at the ambassadorial level. China established diplomatic relations with Saudi Arabia in 1990. China and Israel mutually recognized each other in 1992. By then, China had built up diplomatic relations at the ambassadorial level with all the countries in the Middle East. In 1993, President Jiang Zemin attended the APEC Summit in Seattle and had official and unofficial meetings with more than ten state leaders from Asia and the Pacific region including the US President Clinton. In the following days, President Jiang visited Cuba and Brazil. These visits were the first important diplomatic activities he undertook after he assumed the office of the President of China. The success of the visits not only marked the fact that China had completely broken the impasse in the diplomacy of the early 1990s, but had also ushered in a new era of China's diplomacy.

3. Heads of State Diplomacy: Building a Bridge to the World

A head of a state, the highest leader of a country, is also a final decision-maker for internal and external affairs of that country. Face to face contacts among state leaders not only can avoid entangling technical details by dealing with core issues head on, but also under many circumstances, can dissolve seemingly irreconcilable conflicts of interests through personal friendship.

In the diplomatic history of the People's Republic of China, it is not rare for top leaders to directly participate in diplomatic activities. But President Jiang was the first national leader to have paid so much attention to diplomacy among state leaders, to have met so frequently with foreign heads of state, and to have so effectively promoted the realization of China's diplomatic interests by engaging in activities with the heads of state.

Jiang's presence at the APEC unofficial summit in Seattle in 1993 was his first important diplomatic activity as the President of the state. At the summit, he met with state leaders from Australia, Canada, Indonesia, Japan, Korea,

New Zealand, the Philippines, and the United States. His meeting with President Clinton of the United States was an important event with a bearing on future relations between China and the United States and the stability in Asia and the Pacific region. Jiang's personal characteristics of calmness, intelligence, farsightedness, and humor demonstrated the style of the new generation of the Chinese leaders and caught the attention of public opinion in the world. During the ensuing ten years, while taking part in the annual unofficial APEC summit, meetings of the state leaders of the Shanghai Cooperation Organization, the 50th anniversary of the founding of the United Nations in 1995, and the Millennium Summit of the United Nations in 2000, he visited several dozens of the countries on the five continents. Meanwhile, during this same period he met a great number of state leaders in Beijing.

During the past decade, state diplomacy has made much progress. First, diplomatic contacts with state leaders are effective ways to deal with relations among large countries. In 1993, the talks between Jiang and Clinton in Seattle ended in checking any further deterioration of Sino-US relations. The results would have been unimaginable had there not been direct contacts between the leaders of China and the United States through special envoys or hot line telephone conversations, considering the series of emergency happenings between the two countries such as the crisis across the Taiwan Straits in 1996, the bombing of the Chinese embassy in Yugoslavia in 1999, and the airplane collision in the South China Sea in 2001. Also, without the friendship between Jiang and Yeltsin, China and Russia would have needed much more time to solve the pending issues and to reach strategic cooperation in different areas between the two countries.

Contacts between China and senior-level leaders of European countries and regular summit conferences have laid strong foundations for cooperation between China and the European countries.

Second, diplomatic activities between state leaders have promoted friendship towards neighboring countries and have strengthened China's relations with Third World countries. During the ten years, President Jiang visited all China's neighboring countries and settled the existing issues with most of them. President Jiang placed relations between China and Third World countries at an important place among China's strategies in foreign policy. Through contacts with the state leaders, China has set up all types of strategic cooperation or relations of cooperation with a number of Third World countries.

Third, President Jiang Zemin made contacts with state leaders on different occasions such as the United Nations conferences and APEC conferences. On those occasions, he advocated China's concepts regarding the establishment of a new international political and economic order, multipolarization, elimination of Cold War ways of thinking, and setting up new concepts of security, thus obtaining a prestigious international reputation.

4. Successfully Pulling Through the Financial Crisis

The Asian financial crisis started in Thailand in 1997.
On July 2, 1997, having suffered great losses as a result

of international financial speculators' secret plots and attacks, the Central Bank of Thailand announced that it would abandon the fixed exchange rate that had been practiced for 14 years. The exchange rate for the Baht was then opened to market forces. The following day, the exchange rate of Baht against the US dollar plummeted and by October 31, the Baht had been devaluated by 58.6 percent. After the collapse of the financial market in Thailand, those in the Philippines, Malaysia, and Indonesia also collapsed, throwing those countries into financial crisis. After their success in Southeast Asia, speculators turned to the markets of Taiwan and Hong Kong. On October 7, 1997, Taiwan waived its New Taiwan yuan. The speculators' fund spared no efforts in attacking Hong Kong, (a region that had just returned to the mainland of China), in their attempt to defeat the fixed exchange rate of the HK dollar with the US dollar. With strong countermeasures by the Hong Kong government, the speculators' fund incurred big losses. The fixed exchange rate continued to prevail. However, the stock market in Hong Kong plummeted, especially the assets of four families, such as Li Ka Shing and Kwok Ping Sheung, which shrank by over 50 percent. In November 1997, Korea became another victim of the Asian financial crisis and the Korean Won was devalued by 40 percent. Soon after a famous Japanese security company, Yamaichi, declared bankruptcy. Japan was then on the verge of a financial crisis.

Meanwhile, the international community focused its attention on China and people asked countless questions about whether China would be another victim of the financial crisis. How long could the RMB yuan maintain its value? Would China's economy continue to grow at a fast speed since China's export market was suffering from the crisis?

Since the Chinese financial market was closed to foreign speculators, international financial speculators could not have much impact on the Chinese stock exchange markets. The great devaluation of currencies in Southeast Asian countries, however, still put China into an awkward position. It would have been reasonable for China to devalue the RMB yuan in order to overcome the impact of the currency devaluation in Southeast Asian countries. However, by doing so it would be like dropping stones on those who had fallen into the traps in other Asian countries suffering from a serious financial crisis. Without the devaluation of the RMB yuan, difficulties in China's foreign trade would certainly affect the country's economy, slowing down its growth. While in this dilemma, the Chinese leaders demonstrated again to the world their broadmindedness and far-sightedness. On the mainland, the Chinese government deepened its reform and expanded its domestic demand to encourage economic growth. The Chinese government promised the international community repeatedly that it would maintain the stability of the Chinese currency. With the principle of "sharing weal and woe by proceeding from the same sentiment," China provided assistance through bilateral or multilateral channels to Thailand, Indonesia, and South Korea, contributing its share to the financial and economic stability in Asia and even the world for that matter.

In 1997 and 1998, the Chinese economy maintained its growth rate of 8.8 and 7.8 percent. The country's imports and exports, however, showed stagnation and even decreased. The total import and export volume in 1997 was US $325.1 billion and in 1998 only US $324 billion, showing the first decline since 1983. China succeeded in warding off the financial storm of 1997 by paying a high price.

5. *Fortune*: China and China's Wealth

Fortune is one of the top financial and economic magazines in the world today. Since 1995, it has used its global influence to hold an annual *Fortune* forum, inviting chairmen, presidents, CEOs of transnational corporations, famous world politicians, and celebrities in academic circles to gather at the leading and attractive "hot spot" cities to discuss global economic issues. The first four venues for *Fortune* forums were Singapore in 1995, Barcelona in Spain in 1996, Bangkok in Thailand in 1997, and Budapest in Hungary in 1998.

In 1999, *Fortune* chose Shanghai as the venue for its fifth forum with the theme of "China, the Next 50 Years." The 1999 *Fortune* global forum attracted more than 300 presidents, chairmen and CEOs of transnational corporations, and top managers from over 200 large Chinese enterprises, and more than 800 famous statesmen and scholars from China and other countries and regions in the world. Previous forums had no comparison with this one in terms of scale or level. What was surprising to the world was that this was the first time that *Fortune* focused its theme on one particular country, unlike the previous forums that had placed attention on global issues.

The purpose of the leaders from transnational corporations in attending the 1999 *Fortune* forum was not only to listen to experts expressing their views on the economic development of China in the coming fifty years and to see with their own eyes China's changes during the past twenty years and especially the changes of the previous ten years in Shanghai, but to search for wealth in China and look for a place of their own in China's future development.

The statistics show that at the end of 2000, China had demonstrated the registration of 363,885 enterprises with foreign capital of US $676.097 billion contracted and US $348.346 billion actually used. Since 1993, China has been the second largest recipient of direct foreign investment for nine consecutive years, next only to the United States in the amount of foreign capital attracted. Nearly 400 enterprises out of the world's top 500 enterprises have built plants in China. It is worthwhile to notice that since the mid-1990s, more and more transnational companies have increased their investments in China. Some of them have moved their regional headquarters to China while others have taken China as their production base. Particularly large-size transnational companies such as Motorola, Microsoft and Nokia have set up large-scale R & D centers in China. Obviously China has become the strategic focus for the global operations of the transnational companies. Just as the 1999 *Fortune* forum suggested to all transnational corporations, "They have to compete in China if they want to lead the world."

6. Win-win for China and the WTO

On December 11, 2001, China was formally accepted into the WTO after 15 years of marathon negotiations and 23 years of economic reform. This was perhaps one of the two most important strategic decisions that the Chinese government has made during the last two decades and more.

At the 3rd Plenary Session of the 11th Central Committee of the CPC in 1978, China decided to carry out the policy of reform and opening up to the outside world. The key point of this policy was, according to its own steps, in its own ways, and following its own rules, China would readjust its society that had been closed for a long time. On October 18, 2001, President Jiang spoke at the APEC Meeting of Industrial and Commercial Leaders in Shanghai, saying that: "We are examining and amending existing laws, rules, and regulations according to the requirements of the rules and regulations of the WTO." China had decided to change itself according to the general rules of the WTO for all its members and according to promises China had already made.

Different from the situation in the early days of reform and opening to the outside world, which began in 1978, the compulsory restraints and requests from the outside world would now play an important role in the process of reform after China's accession to the WTO. And the reforms were not only limited to the economic area. China would now bear more pressure for reform in the spheres of law and governmental institutions.

The history of the first thirty years after the founding of the People's Republic of China proved that self-imposed isolation means poverty and backwardness. The reform for more than twenty years proved that to integrate with the outside world is the only way for the Chinese nation to be rejuvenated. China's accession to the WTO is the inevitable outcome of the historical process of China over the past fifty years or more. China's reform has entered a critical period of dealing with the most difficult issues. To some extent, without powerful external pressures, competition, and challenge, it is difficult to make progress in the reform in many areas. Probably the most positive results will emerge twenty years after China's accession to the WTO. According to estimation by the World Bank, if China's promises and reforms are performed as scheduled, China's share in world trade will triple, amounting to 10 percent in 2020. China will import all types of products in large quantities and exports will considerably increase as well. By that time, China will be the second largest exporting country, next only to the United States (the export of the US occupies 12 percent of the total world export), with its exports amounting to 10 percent of the total world export volume, 5 percent higher than those of Japan. If the average compound growth rate predicted by the World Bank is realized, China's aggregate economic strength will increase from 1 percent in 1992 to 4 percent in 2020 of that in the world. If calculated according to the par value of its purchasing power, China will become the second biggest economic entity in the world next to the United States (19 percent), making up 8 percent of the global aggregate economic strength. An official from the WTO has concluded that "China, a country that constantly marches towards powerfulness and prosperity, will bring about great influence to Asia and the world."

The world is pressing China to change dramatically. However, China with a civilization for 5,000 years and a population of one-fifth of the world's total is now undergoing dramatic changes that will surely influence or even change the whole world.

7. New Concept of Security

Since the Cold War ended, the artificial fence separating the people in the East and West has disappeared, and all the countries in the world have the rare opportunity of abandoning the concepts of the Cold War and coming out of the impasse of the traditional concepts of security. With the development of new technologies and the speeding up of globalization, the issue of security that all the countries face has become more complicated. Besides the traditional military security, non-traditional security issues such as economic, financial, and information securities, organized transnational criminal activities, and international terrorism have been disturbing the international community. Therefore, it has become a new issue for all the countries to look for new ways of realizing national security, and to build up a new system of global and regional security.

Chinese leaders have realized that, with the end of the Cold War and speeding up of globalization, the nation now faces a challenge of national security. They are also clearly aware that the traditional concept of security is a threat to global security and stability. Since the mid-1990s, Chinese leaders at different international occasions have emphasized that all countries should abandon their Cold War mentality, build up a new concept of security, and look for new ways to maintain security. The key points of the new concept of security that China advocates are: to build and develop relations among all countries on the basis of the Five Principles of Peaceful Co-existence and to form a stable political basis for global and regional securities; to recognize that all countries should enjoy cooperation and mutual benefits in the economic areas and to be mutually open to each other; to eliminate unequal and discriminative policies in trade relations, gradually narrowing down the gaps between different countries, to seek joint prosperity, and to build up a firm economic basis for global and regional security; and to recognize that all countries should enhance their mutual understanding and trust through dialogue and cooperation, and to promise to settle disputes among countries by peaceful means so that realistic and practical ways can be found to guarantee world peace and security.

At the disarmament conference in Geneva in 1999, President Jiang, in summing up China's practice in foreign policy, spoke about the new concept of security as "mutual trust, benefit, equality, and cooperation" and he stated to the international community China's firm determination to maintain world peace and global security. China is not only an advocator of the new concept of security, but also an implementer.

Since the disintegration of the Soviet Union, the military threats in north and west China have disappeared. However, issues about how to settle the territorial issues left by history; how to control national separatists, religious extremists, and international terrorists; and how to wipe out organized criminal activities such as smuggling and drug trafficking across borders have been discussed by the state leaders of China, Russia, and other newly established Central Asian countries.

Under the joint advocacy and promotion of Sino-Russian leaders, China, Russia, Kazakhstan, Kirghizstan, and Tadzhikistan started negotiations in 1996 on ways to strengthen trust in the military field along the border areas so as to reduce their military forces, and they have formed a system of Shanghai cooperation among the five countries, a model in dealing with the relations among different countries since the end of the Cold War. The leaders from the five countries meet regularly, displaying their far-sightedness, negotiating cooperative areas covering regional security and regional economic cooperation, and especially combating national separatists, international terrorists, and religious extremists. At present, "the Shanghai Five Countries" has become "the

Shanghai Organization of Cooperation" consisting of six countries including Uzbekistan. With the setting up and completion of the system of close cooperation, this new regional organization that seeks security with mutual trust and cooperation through mutual benefit will play an even greater role in the international community.

8. A Power Engine, Not a Trap in Asia

Since China successfully withstood the Asian financial crisis and joined the WTO, comments from the West have been contradictory: Some people have predicted that China's advantageous position in competition, which has been gradually built up in Asia, will eventually outdo Japan's economy, will squeeze the United States out of East Asia, and even replace its economic influence there; others have predicted that China's economy will totally collapse due to its inability to adapt to dramatic changes and fierce competition after its accession to the WTO.

In theory, many countries in Asia are short of capital and technology, just as China is, and have product structures similar to that in China. Thus they and China all target North America, Japan, and Europe as their major export markets. Therefore, with China's entry into the WTO, competition is intensified. Generally speaking, many countries in Asia do not have the same comparable advantages that China does such as salary level, quality of labor power, and market potential. It is, therefore, expected that within a certain period of time capital, technology, market shares, and related industries will shift to China.

This way of thinking, however, has a fundamental fault since, in the first place, it negates the positive effect brought about by competition and denies that active participation in competition may result in the early arrival of, and on an even larger scale, an industrial revolution in the region. Second, it overlooks the fact that China's increase in trade is not only an expansion of its exports but may well be an expansion of imports too. An economist with Goldman Sachs stationed in Hong Kong believes that since China's accession to the WTO, the country's annual import growth rate will increase from the present 7 percent to 12 percent. The World Bank estimates that in the coming twenty years, China's growing imports will make up 40 percent of the total import growth of all developing countries. Third, studies of the data from 34 countries between 1985 and 1999 made by Mr. Huang, an economist with Salomon Smith Barney, indicate that the increase in China's direct foreign investment was in proportion with the increase of foreign investments in other Northeast Asian and the Southeast Asian countries. In other words, the speedy growth of the Chinese economy may well lead to more international capital being put into the countries and regions with close economic ties with China. Finally, at a time when contacts among the countries are becoming increasingly close, it is hard to imagine one country is booming in its economy, while its neighbors are in ruins.

Fortunately, leaders of the Asian countries do not regard China's economy and its accession to the WTO as pitfalls. Instead, with a more open and confident attitude, they look to China as another valuable opportunity. Further, Chinese leaders are determined to share the fruits of their economic takeoff with their neighbors. Economic cooperation along the Mekong River is already showing initial results and negotiations for the ASEAN-China Free Trade Zone have begun. The prospect of a joint takeoff by China and its Asian neighbors is already within sight.

9. A Big, Responsible Country

China's aggregate economic strength is only one-ninth that of the United States and a quarter that of Japan. In fact, China is even lagging behind many developing nations. Economically speaking, China is not a strong country. Even if the development goals set by Deng Xiaoping can be realized in the mid-21st century, and even if China really can catch up with Japan or the United States in the next thirty to fifty years, or less, as suggested by many authoritative institutions, China today is at most a potential power.

China, however, is one of the five permanent members of the UN Security Council and a major member of the world's nuclear club. China has a population of 1.3 billion and it is the sixth largest economy in the world. The country is also the sixth largest trading nation in the world. In the last twenty years or more, the Chinese economy has grown at an annual rate of 9 percent. It is apparent that in the eyes of the world, China is undoubtedly a big country. To be a big and responsible country has always been an important goal of China's diplomacy.

In the summer of 1997, a financial crisis swept across East Asia. In order to prevent the situation from worsening, China, with tremendous courage, maintained the value of its Renminbi, thus contributing to reigning in the crisis from further spread and worsening against its own huge economic loss. In 1998, India and Pakistan competed in conducting nuclear tests, suddenly intensifying the nuclear arms race in South Asia and confronting the global nuclear non-proliferation system with the danger of total failure. China took quick action in the UN Security Council by actively contacting the United States and together they presided over a meeting of the five permanent members of the Security Council, which resulted in a communiqué by the foreign ministers. On this basis, the resolutions passed by the United Nations urged all countries concerned to go with the tide of the time, abandon their nuclear weapons programs, and unconditionally sign the *Comprehensive Nuclear Test Ban Treaty* and the *Treaty on the Non-proliferation of Nuclear Weapons*. These diplomatic efforts taken by China won wide acclaim. China's international image as a large, peace-loving, cooperative, and responsible country has been widely recognized by the international community.

China's rise is irresistible and it is a historical inevitability for China to play an increasingly important role in international affairs. It should be remembered, however, that to be a large country has its price. As a large country with great potential, China should perform the obligations and duties appropriate to its strength. Meanwhile, there are huge gaps between China's historical experience and cultural accumulation over the last several thousand years and the generally accepted practices and ways of behavior in the world today. Consequently, China should study and learn how to help reform and improve the international system that was established in contemporary times mostly on the basis of the Western cultural background. What should be pointed out is that a big country not only should have the backup of powerful military and economic strength, it should also build a cultural atmosphere of a cohesive and attractive political system as well as an impressive code of ethics. To establish an image of being a big and responsible nation, China still has a long way to go.

10. To Be Wise: Suiting One's Actions to the Times

One of the important trends in the world today is globalization. Though the debate on globalization has become global itself, there are some solid facts that cannot be challenged: the process of globalization is speeding up; globalization means the strengthening of relations and mutual dependence among the countries; the impact of globalization has gone beyond the economic sphere, and the changes brought about by globalization are only beginning to become evident.

For a given country, these basic facts mean that globalization is an irresistible and unavoidable historic process. To take part in globalization is the only choice available.

In correspondence with globalization, regional integration is the second trend of our time. In Europe, the EU has set up an example of integration for the world. In North America, the United States is working hard on developing a North American Free Trade Zone. Besides, regional cooperation organizations can be found just about everywhere in the world. Whatever the initial targets of these organizations, and no matter how different they are from each other in their functions and roles, they have demonstrated some common features in the last decade and more. For all the participants, an integrated organization is not only a bastion against global risks, but also provides a springboard and supports in obtaining better conditions for taking part in globalization.

Globalization has brought closer ties and speedy changes. The interests of different nations are not only pluralistic but are hard to distinguish or separate in many aspects. Thus the risks in decision-making have increased and the harm done by wrong decisions has become serious. This requires that the decision makers of all nations be scientifically sound, democratic, and reasonable. They must give more consideration to the interests and stances of other countries. International political democratization has become another great trend and direction of our time.

Chinese leaders are fully aware of the three great trends and their impact on China. Through accession to the WTO, China has demonstrated its boldness and confidence in taking part in global competition. Meanwhile, the country is increasingly aware of the significance of regional cooperative organizations for China's economy, politics, and security. China is one of the most active APEC members, has reached common understanding with ASEAN to establish a free trade zone, and has hosted the establishment of the Shanghai Cooperation Organization. China has also given great attention to the economic cooperation along the Mekong River and in Northeast Asia. As for international political democratization, China has long been an advocate of multilateralism. Several thousand years ago, Confucius had already said: "Do not do to others what you would not have them do to you."

(Written by Zhao Xiaodong)

About the writers

Li Ping is a research fellow and deputy director of the Quantity Economy and Technological Economy Research Institute and deputy director for the Research and Consulting Center of Project Estimation and Strategic Planning, the Chinese Academy of Social Sciences. He has taken part in several major national economic research and forecasting projects, feasibility studies, project debates, and verification programs for three national cross-century projects, namely the Three Gorges Project, the South-North Water Diversion Project, and the Beijing-Shanghai Express Railway Project, as well as the appraisal of several infrastructure and foreign investment projects. He has furthermore undertaken the mapping of several departmental and regional strategic plans. He has also provided consulting services to enterprises in their management, development strategy, and investment projects.

Zhang Yi, from Jingning, Gansu, was born in December 1964 and has his MA degree in sociology. Now he is an associate research fellow, professor in the MA program, and deputy director of the Population and Social Development Research Office, Population Studies Institute of the Chinese Academy of Social Sciences. He has published in leading national newspapers and journals including *China Social Sciences* (Chinese and foreign language editions) *China Population Science, Sociology Studies, East, Reading,* and the *Guangming Daily*. Recent books he has published include *The Trend of Family Ownership and Management of State-owned Enterprises*, *An Analysis of the Social Cost of State-owned Enterprises* (co-author), and *System Changes and Labor Employment* (co-author). His articles and books have won national book awards, a prize for scientific research issued by the Chinese Academy of Social Sciences and a prize for national population scientific research achievements.

Zhou Mansheng is research fellow and deputy director of the State Education Development Research Center of the Ministry of Education, professor of the Ph.D program at Beijing Normal University, a member of the leading group for National Educational Science Planning, a member of the National Education and Self-taught Examination Research Committee, China Education Society, and China Education Science Committee, and a council member of China Comparative Education Society. He has long been engaged in the research of macro-education policies and comparative education research, and has taken part in the drafting of the national macro-education policy and regulations. He has served as a research project team member and consulting specialist for UNESCO and the Asian Development Bank. He presided over a key research project of the Ministry of Education during the Ninth Five-year Plan period called the "Basic Characteristics and Rules of World Education Reform and Development in the 1990s" and a key research project of philosophy and social science for the Tenth Five-year Plan period called "A Comparative Study of Educational Macro-policies."

Tang Jun received his MA in applied social science from

Hong Kong University of Technology in 1996 and is now a Ph.D candidate. He is also an associate research fellow and deputy director of the Social Policy Research Center of the Chinese Academy of Social Sciences. Since 1986, he has been engaged in the study of applied social science, completing more than twenty topics, including nine key national research projects and Ministry of Civil Affairs projects. He has published books and articles totaling more than 2 million characters and 80,000 characters in translation.

Zhang Shifei is a staff member with the Social Policy Research Center of the Sociology Research Institute of the Chinese Academy of Social Sciences, and a Ph.D graduate in social welfare. In recent years, he has published several papers in the *Hong Kong Social Work Journal* and in the *Hong Kong Social Science Journal*.

Wang Yanzhong, with a Ph.D in sociology from Peking University, is a visiting scholar in economics at Oxford University, a research fellow and deputy director of the Scientific Research Bureau, a professor in the Industrial Economics Department of the Graduate School, deputy council chairman of the WTO Research Center, and member of the Chinese Academy of Social Sciences. He has also been a special guest research fellow at the Social Securities Research Institute of the Labor and Social Security Ministry, and an executive council member of the China Social Security Society. He focuses his research on industrial economics, development strategy for small and medium-size enterprises and labor and social security. His major works include *WTO and the Development Strategy for Small and Medium-size Enterprises, Economic Organizations and Urban and Rural*

Development, and *Report on the Development of Social Securities in China* (co-author). He has organized and participated in more than twenty Chinese and foreign research projects and drawn up more than ten strategic development plans for localities and enterprises.

Shen Jie, with a Ph.D in sociology, is an associate research fellow of the Sociology Research Institute of the Chinese Academy of Social Sciences, and a member of the International Sociology Association. His areas of research are social development and psychology. He has taken part in and presided over more than ten major research projects of the country, the Chinese Academy of Social Sciences, and various ministries such as the ones that produced "A Study of China's Social Changes" and "Social Psychology during the Period of Transition of the Social Structure." His paper entitled "The Formation of Social Adhesiveness During the Transition of China's Social Structure" won the prize for excellence at the Competition of Research Papers of World Young Sociologists. His books *Theories of Social Psychology* and *Modern Applied Social Psychology* have been awarded academic prizes.

Wang Chunfa, a native of Rushan, Shandong, was born in November 1963. With a Ph.D in economics he was recently a visiting scholar at George Washington University in the United States. Now he is a research fellow and director of the World Industrial Structure Research Office of the World Economy and Politics Research Institute, professor of the MA program, at the Chinese Academy of Social Sciences, vice executive council chairman of the China Science and Technology Policy Research Society, member of the special committee of the Chinese Youth Creation Forum/Zhongguancun Science Park Forum, and a member of the editorial committees of *World Economy and Politics* and *Science and Technology Management*.

Liu Zhiyan, born in 1967, finished his studies for an economics post-doctoral program of the Chinese Academy of Social Sciences. Now an associate research fellow and deputy director of the Urban Economics Office, he is also a professor in the MA program at the Chinese Academy of Social Sciences. His studies are focused on environmental, regional and urban economies. He has participated in and presided over several research projects of key national science and technology programs, the State Natural Science Foundation, National Social Science Foundation, and various government ministries, as well as projects to draw up development strategies for more than twenty cities. He has written a series of books and published more than thirty research papers.

Zhang Guanxin, a native of Cangshan, Shandong, was born in August 1966. He is a member of the All-China Youth Federation. He is also an associate research fellow and assistant director of the General Affairs Office of the Leading Party Group of the Chinese Academy of Social Sciences, deputy executive council chairman and secretary-general of the Youth Humanity and Social Science Research Center, and a member of the post-doctoral program of the Law Institute at the Chinese Academy of Social Sciences. His areas of study are traditional legal culture and the legal anthropology of ethnic minorities.

图书在版编目（CIP）数据

中国现代化——对中国百姓及经济发展的影响 /北京青年报社，
中国社会科学院青年人文社会科学研究中心主编；
郝光锋等译．
一北京：外文出版社，2004
ISBN 7-119-03297-6
I. 中… II. ①北… ②中… ③郝… III. 社会调查－调查报告－中国－英文
IV. D668

中国版本图书馆 CIP 数据核字（2003）第 013574 号

| 英文审定 | 黄友义　卓科达 | 封面设计 | 蔡　荣 |
| 执行编辑 | 杨春燕 | 印刷监制 | 张国祥 |

中国现代化——对中国百姓及经济发展的影响

北京青年报社

中国社会科学院青年人文社会科学研究中心　主编

英　译

郝光锋　孔伟　丛国龄　路江

*

©外文出版社
外文出版社出版
（中国北京百万庄大街 24 号）
邮政编码　100037
外文出版社网址：www.flp.com.cn
外文出版社电子信箱：info@flp.com.cn
sales@flp.com.cn

三河汇鑫印务有限公司印刷
中国国际图书贸易总公司发行
（中国北京车公庄西路 35 号）
北京邮政信箱第 399 号　邮政编码　100044
2004 年（小 16 开）第 1 版
2004 年 3 月第 1 版第 1 次印刷
（英）
ISBN 7-119-03297-6/Z 635（外）
04600（平）
17-E-3544 P